First Published November 1989 by Tribute Book Pty. Limited, Australia
Copyright © 1989 Tribute Book Pty. Limited

Published in the United States of America by Tribute Book Pty. Limited
15 Bourke Street, Woolloomooloo, New South Wales, 2011 Australia

Produced by Jones & Janello, New York
Design by Beth A. Crowell
Computer composed mechanicals by Mark F. Cheung
Police Interviews by Paul McIver and Neil Lawrence

Printed in the United States of America by Southeastern Printing

ISBN 0 7316 8126 6

10 9 8 7 6 5 4 3 2 1

Tribute

A Day on the Beat with America's Finest

Created and developed by

Neil Lawrence
Paul McIver
John Henderson
Norm Croker

in cooperation with the

Police Executive Research Forum

Produced and edited by Jones & Janello, New York
Designed by Beth A. Crowell

A Note about the Book

In the summer of 1985 a young Australian freelance photographer was touring the United States when his imagination was captured by a burning idea. He had become fascinated with the U.S. police officers he encountered as he roamed the country. He decided, then and there, to create a book that would show America's police in all their color and diversity — warts and all. Paul McIver spent the next four years living and photographing his dream. Along the way, he came to realize that, given this nation's size, the true dimensions of its police could not be easily squeezed through one photographer's lens in much less than a lifetime. He also concluded that for the dream to succeed and do justice to American police officers, a battle plan was needed that would tap both creative talent and financial acumen. The young Australian turned to three of his fellow countrymen, John Henderson, Neil Lawrence, and Norm Croker, and to Englishman Jim Henderson, for these skills.

The group quickly concluded that the book would excel if a balanced, respected, and independent police body supported the project and helped the team gain the fullest access to U.S. police departments. An American colleague, Nate Rosenblatt, introduced them to the Washington-based Police Executive Research Forum (PERF) and its executive director, Darrel Stephens. What started as an exploratory conversation between Lawrence and Stephens swiftly evolved into a full-scale cooperative effort — a venture that saw Lawrence and Stephens (a former chief of police himself) in constant communication between Washington and Sydney, structuring the project and laying the groundwork for the editorial challenges that lay ahead.

So successful was PERF's role in planning and making introductions to police that a six-week photographic shoot by Paul McIver and fellow Australian photojournalist Peter Hendrie, undertaken at a breakneck pace throughout America, never fell behind, except for one afternoon. (And that was because the two lensmen were involved in a fender bender in Philadelphia!)

After the initial shooting, the Australian group invited nearly a dozen of America's premier photojournalists to join them on police assignment U.S.A.

The results of all this Australian-American planning and creativity is the book you hold in your hands, *Tribute: A Day on the Beat with America's Finest*. It is perhaps the most intimate and comprehensive portrait of U.S. police officers ever produced.

The book opens with a no-nonsense introduction about American police life by Darrel Stephens, who writes with an affection and a critical eye that only a seasoned law enforcement veteran could achieve.

Tribute's main chapters document a twenty-four-hour day with police officers around the nation. The story begins with roll call in a New York City Police Department and ends, twenty-four cities later, with a SWAT team of the Honolulu Police Department. Along the way, photographs and personal reflections by officers themselves reveal the many facets of police life.

A "Legends and Heroes" chapter profiles twenty-four extraordinary police officers who were singled out by their departments for mention in this book. The officers were selected from a large group of entries, all of whom should be honored. Some were chosen for single acts of heroism or bravery, some for years of extraordinary service, and others for sacrificing their lives in the line of duty.

A final chapter, "Policing the Future," acknowledges past and current police practices and gazes ahead at the obstacles and opportunities that confront America's police.

At the back of the book is a list of acknowledgments to the dozens of people who contributed their time and energy to make *Tribute* a success. Without the tremendous support and commitment of the staff and leadership of PERF itself, the book would not have been created. In thanks and recognition of their role, royalties from every book sold will be donated through PERF to the National Law Enforcement Memorial Fund and other appropriate groups.

■

It should be noted that the personal reflections and photographs in *Tribute* are intended to create an impressionistic portrait of a police officer's life and that no specific relationship exists between individual photographs and text. Most of *Tribute*'s photographs document actual policework and events. Others capture police training and exercises. A few images in the book — those on pages 92, 95, 113, 115 and 213 — are simulations of particular law enforcement situations.

The text consists of excerpts from extended conversations with police officers in the twenty-four cities on which the book focuses. The individual voices of the officers are separated by square bullets in the text. The opinions expressed by these police are their own and not necessarily those of the departments in which they serve.

Introduction

Americans have a fascination with police that is tireless. Criminals and the cops pursuing them are the flesh and blood of countless bestsellers, and the television and motion picture industries are practically fueled by tales of police life and the smooth and rough-edged people that cops encounter. When most of us are out driving, the sight of a police cruiser triggers a simultaneous check of the speedometer and a lifting of the foot on the accelerator. When we need assistance, the police are the first people we dial. And yet the public's perception of law enforcement officials is a highly contradictory one — part threatening, part security symbol. In most instances, that view is shaped by surprisingly little solid knowledge of the men and women who arouse these emotions and the reality of their work.

Who, in fact, *is* the real cop? The one who relentlessly pursues the criminal? The one who risks a career by cutting corners to bypass "out of touch" police administrators and courts that seem to protect criminals at the expense of the victim? The potbellied cop who hangs around a donut shop and delights in using his

authority to bully kids who are just having a good time? Or is it Norman Rockwell's picture of goodness who sits at the soda fountain with the runaway kid? Watch the evening news to see the police officer depicted as either corrupt, brutal, and racist or a true American hero who risks his or her life for what is good and decent.

Not surprisingly, the police embody a bit of all these images. After all, close to 500,000 of them serve in about 17,000 agencies that range in size from New York City, with almost 28,000 police officers, to small towns with as few as one. About 80 percent of American police departments employ fewer than ten full-time officers. Although it's changing, policework is a predominantly white male occupation. Women constitute 8 percent, blacks about 9, Hispanics 5 and other minorities one. Currently, 45 percent of America's police have two or more years of college, compared to only 10 percent in 1960. Obviously, with close to a half million officers serving in thousands of departments nationwide, officers can be found that personify both the positive and the negative images broadcast and perpetuated by the media.

Rarely, however, do these polar images reflect the full range of activities that engage the police officer. Nor do they reveal the range of emotions that an officer feels while on duty. In fact, the professional image of the police officer would suggest that many of these emotions are improper. Moreover, most of what the media reports about police focuses on their on-duty activities and seldom reveals the effects of the job on their families. To be sure, a police officer faces the same financial and personal problems common to most American families. Like them, both partners in the marriage work demanding jobs, and it's not unusual for the officer to hold a second, part-time job. But they have special pressures on them as well. Shift schedules that are constantly changing and exceedingly long work hours make them scramble to squeeze in attendance at their children's school and recreational activities. Almost chronically, they end up missing key family events and holidays because of police duties. This only adds to the normal stresses and strains created by a police officer's life.

Policework imposes special responsibilities on the officer's family as well. Even though they never took oaths of police service, in the eyes of many, their actions are judged as critically as those of the officer himself. They all must be above reproach in their personal conduct. They can never allow themselves to get in situations that generate comments like, "If your dad saw us doing this, he would arrest all of us." And in a cop's family, a simple question like, "What did you do at work today?" is one that the police officer is often not allowed to answer. The day's events just might be too gory or too confidential to be shared. This confidentiality can cause family members to feel cut off and isolated from the police officer's world. It is, indeed, an enormous sacrifice that the police officer and his or her family make when they pledge to serve their community. But fortunately, for whatever reasons, they keep on doing it.

Police officers frequently see individuals at their worst. They are constantly summoned to people's homes to help settle disputes involving the most personal of matters. Over time, officers can become a bit cynical and distrustful, a mind-set that can also spill over into their family lives making them overly protec-

tive of their children and, perhaps, more suspicious and wary than the average parent.

Another dimension of the police officer's life involves the tool of his trade — the gun. Although an essential part of American law enforcement, it is a constant reminder of the continuing threat of violence that officers face. Some departments require their officers to carry firearms at all times. Many do it voluntarily

fearing they will encounter off duty the kinds of criminals they routinely meet on the job. They also do it to protect themselves from the risk of personal vendettas by criminals they've arrested in the past.

Why would anyone choose this occupation? Why do they go through the months of arduous intellectual and physical training to become a cop? Why do they so readily suffer the verbal abuse of a sometimes ungrateful public, and the physical abuse of street patrol in the climatic extremes of winter and summer? And why do they give themselves over to a job that taxes their social and mental skills every working hour and still requires their total psychological commitment twenty-four hours a day? The answer to this question is as varied as the personalities of American

police officers themselves. Some officers follow in their fathers' footsteps. Others are drawn to the image of the good guys defeating the bad. Not until later do they discover how difficult it is to sort out the good from the bad. Studies suggest that many choose law enforcement because it is perceived to be a profession that helps people. Still others are attracted to it because of the relative job security. Regardless of the reasons, it is to these men and women that this book pays tribute.

The officers who patrol this nation's streets and highways are indeed our unsung heroes — America's finest. They work the toughest hours and respond to the meanest calls. They are the ones who go face to face with our worst living nightmares in the dead of night. And they are the ones who look after the alcoholic and the mentally disabled in a society that feels good about itself because it decriminalized the former and deinstitutionalized the latter — but never quite got around to replacing the jails with adequate treatment facilities. The police are the ones who live firsthand "man's inhumanity to man." They are the bearers of bad news to shattered parents when tragedy descends on their children. And they are also the ones who must say something soothing when confronted with the hurt and confusion of a child who can't understand why daddy beat mommy. Police officers often walk the worst beats of life — among the people and places where the American dream has never been realized. Yet they continue to respond. They continue to make a difference in a world where they are sometimes viewed as the bad guys. To be sure, a few are not suited for the authority and trust that go with their badges. But most are conscientious and committed officers who do a difficult and dangerous job — a job that is vital to society but often taken for granted. It is to them that this book is dedicated.

— Darrel Stephens

Roll Call

32nd Precinct, Harlem, New York, New York

"Policework can quickly turn from hours of boredom to minutes of sheer terror. You could be doing something as ordinary as writing a parking ticket or simply walking the beat. One split second later, you find yourself face to face with some guy running out of a store with a shotgun."

T he police officer's shift begins with roll call. It's like taking a head count, the time we check to see that the cops who are scheduled to be on duty have actually shown up. Thing's move fast around here, and officers often get shifted to other platoons. Or at a moment's notice, they might get sent off to court or on special assignment. Roll call's kind of a reality check so we know for certain who's where. An often repeated quip is that you sign out of roll call at the end of the day. As long as you have a beginning and an end to roll call, then you have had a good day.

If a cop is scheduled for the shift and hasn't turned up at roll call, we look to find out why. Did this person get involved in an incident or get hurt on the way to work? If something special's happened around the precinct, roll call's the place to make the officers aware of it. It's also a dress inspection, to make sure our appearance is up. We're going to be out there dealing with the public.

Roll call's also the place that we hammer into the officers' heads that they need to wear their bullet-resistant vests. When I inspect the platoon and open up the ranks, I check carefully that each officer is wearing that vest. These things save lives! On a hot summer day, cops get lax. They don't want to wear them. But we're losing too many officers to gunfire. They've just got to keep them on at all times.

We also repeatedly stress teamwork at roll call. For most of these guys it's almost instinctive — the need to back each other up when the going gets tough. There's great camaraderie, and the officers tend to protect each other. When someone calls for help, shots have been fired, or somebody gets stabbed, there is quick backup because each officer knows how slow time passes when you need help.

Unfortunately, we get more than our fair share of just these kinds of urgent calls. Each precinct has it's own special problems and crime patterns. It may be inordinately high numbers of stolen cars or serious assaults. It might just be too many jaywalkers. But

"Roll call's kind of a reality check so we know for certain who's where ... We also repeatedly stress teamwork at roll call. For most of these guys it's almost instinctive — the need to back each other up when the going gets tough."

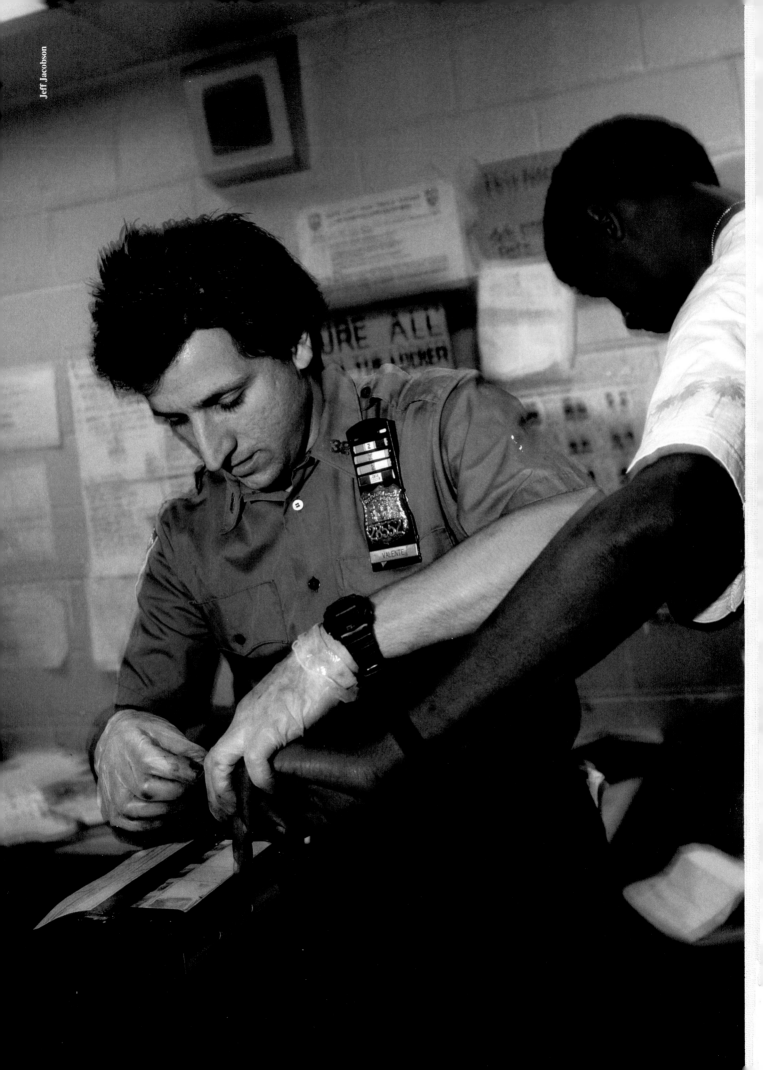

Jeff Jacobson

here it's an infestation of narcotics and drug trafficking and the violence it breeds.

Policework can quickly turn from hours of boredom to minutes of sheer terror. You could be doing something as ordinary as writing a parking ticket or simply walking the beat. One split second later, you find yourself face to face with some guy running out of a store with a shotgun. You've got to be smart, have your wits about you, and know how to make the right decisions — and fast! Despite the terror and all that adrenaline, you've got to act cool and cautious and take into account the safety of your partner and members of the community. You've even got to think about the safety of the perpetrator himself. It's serious work, a real tough job.

■

This is one of the most violent precincts in the world. Perhaps it's the worst! We've had sixty-five homicides so far this year and I guess it will be up to eighty-five by the end of the year. That's more than twice the homicide rate for most European countries! And you have to remember that's only the dead. It doesn't even include the wounded. The hospital here is so accustomed to violent injuries that sometimes it looks like a MASH unit.

With all this activity going on, we need to keep our officers informed of violent trends and other good news. That's where roll call comes in. It's a head-counting exercise and a total briefing and debriefing session.

Once we've got the officers assembled, we let them know what's up. Recently we had a couple of guys hailing cabs at Penn Station and then bringing them to Harlem and robbing them. There was also a recent spate of people throwing bricks off roofs. We share information, tell them how to deal with this stuff.

Just a couple of days ago, we checked out an apartment where the officers couldn't gain access but they could smell the unmistakable odor of death. They went around back, saw a body on the floor, and forced their way through a window next to the fire escape. The apartment had been ransacked, and the old woman on the floor had multiple stab wounds. Her husband's body was discovered in the next room, also with stab wounds.

The officers called the precinct to report a double homicide. When we go through an investigation, it's a thoroughly painstaking process. We move slowly so as not to miss anything. It was only a little over two hours later that a young officer found a third body in similar condition under a bed. It was another elderly woman who had evidently tried to protect herself by crawling under there.

This all happened only about one block away from the precinct. In some ways roll call allows us older heads to put this kind of thing in perspective for officers like the youngster who found the third body. This is a tough job in a tough precinct. Roll call is our family meet. We're in this together.

■

How to avoid wrapping the patrol car around a fire hydrant on the way to a crime — that's a typical problem that gets aired at roll call. Cops are always getting hurt responding to an officer's call for assistance or to a heavy job, like a robbery, where shots are being fired. The adrenaline gets pumping, and some officers drive themselves right into an accident, even before they get to the scene. We try to tell them, "You're no help to anyone if you don't get there." That's one of the major things that's stressed.

Sometimes people say the Harlem community's not too supportive of us, but it's not true. The majority of the people here want police protection. Most of the older Harlem residents relate to us better than the younger ones. The older people have lived here for years. They remember Harlem when it was a thriving community with lots of nightclubs. This was once a happening area of town, and they cherish that memory. But many of the kids have no respect for the police. Drugs are on every other block, and the young people who are dealing them make immense amounts of money. They are constantly competing with each other, often violently. Sometimes it

seems there's little we can do about the drugs. But we hear about them constantly from the community itself. They know where the problems are. They know who's dealing drugs, and they tell us. Usually our undercover cops get on it.

Working in a busy precinct is not like walking the beat in some other low-crime area of the city. You need constant input. You need to know what's happening on the street. You ask cops on the shift before you what's happening. And you're constantly turning to your sources on the street. Out on patrol, officers even get in a huddle sometimes, just to share information on this block or that, and to warn each other that bottles are being thrown off the roof on that building down the way.

The police department attracts a lot of young people because the money's good and the retirement benefits are attractive. I joined the police when I was twenty years old, and if everything works out, I'm going to retire when I am forty. I'm already considered a veteran on this job, having put in only five years of service. In the old days, I'd still be considered a rookie even with ten years. But right now, with 75 percent of the officers having five years or less experience, I'm a senior man.

Traffic Accidents

New York State Police, Albany, New York

"When the police arrive at the scene of an accident, people are happy to see us, because we're authority — someone to take control of what can be a frightening and chaotic situation."

Here's your typical car accident around here. Cars are heading in opposite directions, and one decides to make a left-hand turn through the path of oncoming traffic. The driver thinks it's clear sailing and takes a shot at it, only to find he misjudged completely. He's failed to give adequate right-of-way to a vehicle approaching fast from the opposite direction, and…kaabang! There's your routine traffic accident! Most of them are avoidable. The guy's rushing, thinking he can shave off five minutes by cutting corners and taking shortcuts. If he'd only left a little earlier, a fender bender wouldn't have occurred.

When we first arrive at the scene of a car accident, we make sure the people aren't injured, and that nobody's going to either pass out or pass away while we're there. Fortunately, we're seeing fewer cuts and bruises, because New York State now requires seat belts. They've definitely helped reduce injuries! We then get the vehicles off the road so the traffic can begin moving smoothly again and so we don't risk getting hit. The last thing we want to contend with as we're sorting things out is a major traffic jam breeding gawkers and other minor accidents. Then we get on with the investigation — check driver's licenses and registrations, talk with witnesses, and try to determine fault. Usually you can see from the accident itself who was at fault. It always helps to have a witness confirm it.

When the police arrive at the scene of an accident, people are happy to see us, because we're authority — someone to take control of what can be a frightening and chaotic situation. Most times, people are arguing and fussing back and forth, blaming each other for the damage, and nothing's really getting resolved on its own. Often, someone's really hyper, so you give 'em time to calm down a bit.

■

Only now, two years after the accident, did they discover the last body, almost seventy miles from the scene. It was a bridge collapse

and the worst accident I've ever worked on. It was like a national disaster, with ten people killed. The bridge was on Interstate 90, the New York State Thruway, and spanned Schoharie Creek. After the collapse it took nearly a year to restore the road to normal.

I arrived at the site of the accident only hours after it fell. The torrential rains before, during, and after the accident posed horrendous problems. It was like a scene from a disaster movie, with utter chaos and destruction and emergency service people arriving from all directions. The search and rescue operation involved boats, scuba divers, helicopters, investigation units, traffic rerouting, two separate units of state troopers, foot and mounted patrols, identification patrols, and more media personnel than you could poke a stick at. Just to complicate matters, rubberneckers were crawling out of the woodwork. Hoards of them were out there in inclement weather just gawking. We had our hands full just keeping them away.

Within a short space of time, we'd set up a temporary, state-of-the-art, high-tech command post at the site of the accident. The recovery and investigation operations went on for weeks. Even the media were using satellite dishes and technology I had not seen before. It was mostly harrowing and very hard work. The tragedy created a strong sense of family amongst everyone involved, particularly with all of us police working our days off and long hours in hazardous and strenuous conditions. It proved to me that when the need is there, we can rise to the occasion.

■

Our officers don't usually get traumatized by serious incidents like gruesome fatalities or toxic waste spillage. We get six months of extensive training at the police academy during which we learn how to cope with tragedies. Troopers are shown films and taken to hospital emergency rooms. They observe autopsies. Once they get out on the street, they should be able to think clearly and respond effectively in even the most catastrophic situations.

The worst aspect of rush-hour accidents tends to be the inconvenience they cause to other motorists on the highway. Commuters heading into the city are delayed and arrive late for work. Some businesses won't open on time. Often secondary accidents occur, especially chain reactions with drivers rear-ending each other. If traffic gets bottled up completely, it wreaks havoc on emergency vehicles, delaying the arrival of ambulances, fire trucks, and special service units.

We've started to rise above that problem by using helicopters — particularly to medivac the injured from remote areas or where there is highly congested traffic. In addition, some of our state troopers are now trained medical technicians and have cars equipped with the essentials for providing emergency care at the scene of an accident.

We're seeing more and more accidents on our highways. The surge of residential development throughout the state is the major culprit, especially growth in the major metropolitan areas. You have to remember the state police primarily patrol rural state areas and the burgeoning suburbs. We don't patrol in the major cities or towns of the state. But we do maintain interstate or highway patrols on roads that pass through those jurisdictions. Albany and the capital district have experienced a tremendous increase in the number of residential developments over the past ten to fifteen years. A significant growth of traffic on our roads in these areas is a direct result of this growth. It's a challenge for us, particularly in winter, when we get severe weather on a regular basis.

One of the road accidents we had today was a minor one involving an illegally registered truck that had no insurance and was using another vehicle's license plates. It was a dump truck and carrying a load of hot asphalt. With a truck like that, the accident could have been much worse. A similar one actually flipped in such an incident some time ago, and a woman driving by was entombed in tons of 300-degree asphalt. Due to the heroic efforts of some people at the scene, she was literally dug out of her car before she succumbed to the

" If a child or his parents are injured in a car crash, it can be terrifying. For most, it is the first traumatic experience of their life. The arrival of a big state trooper and all the flashing lights might, momentarily, make it seem even more frightening. Getting the child calmed down and relaxed and getting him to trust the officer are among our first concerns."

fumes and heat. If a vehicle is carrying dangerous cargo, tragic consequences can be triggered by even the smallest of accidents.

Usually, we are a very welcome sight at the scene of an accident or other road problem. In most cases, people have an immediate need for our help, whether it's giving first aid, getting a tow truck, collecting essential information, or simply calming people and putting them at ease. Many of the calls we get are not very exciting. For example, a person can't change a flat tire or do minor repairs under the hood. Our troopers are all trained in basic mechanical skills, and we are in touch with a fleet of commercially sponsored service vehicles known as the Roadside Samaritans. They're radio-equipped service vans that respond when someone is needed to change a flat tire, gas an empty tank, or fix a radiator hose or fan belt, free of charge.

Our troopers are especially concerned about the welfare of children at the scene of an accident. If a child or his parents are injured in a car crash, it can be terrifying. For most, it is the first traumatic experience of their life. The arrival of a big state trooper and all the flashing lights might, momentarily, make it seem even more frightening. Getting the child calmed down and relaxed and getting him to trust the officer are among our first concerns.

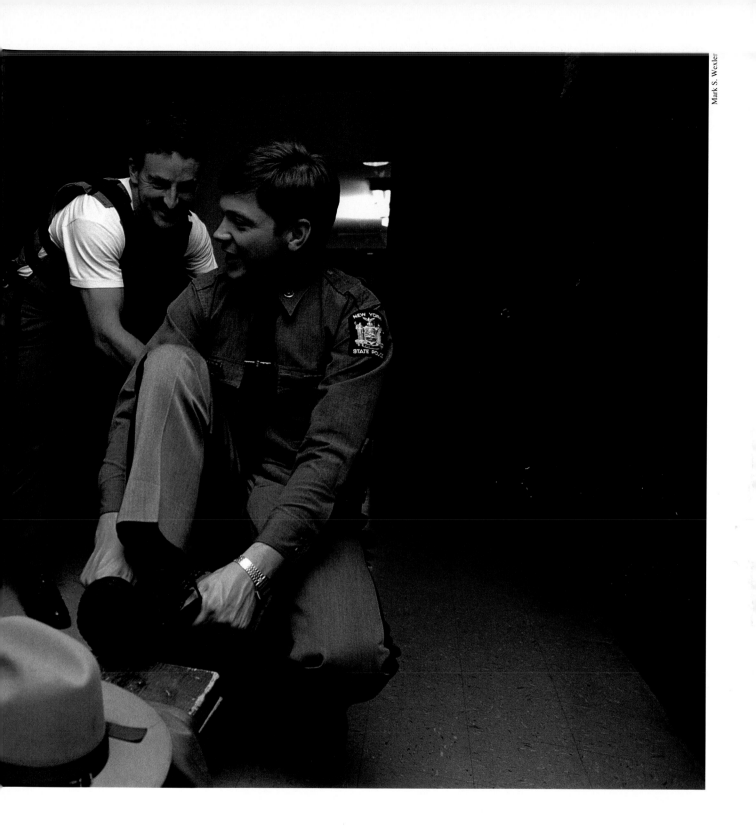

*"It was a bridge collapse and the worst accident I've ever worked on...
The tragedy created a strong sense of family amongst everyone involved, particularly with all of us police
working our days off and long hours in hazardous and strenuous conditions. It proved to me that
when the need is there, we can rise to the occasion."*

Business Burglary

Philadelphia, Pennsylvania

"You're apprehensive. You're a little scared. You anticipate the very worst, just to be on the safe side. You just know the thief isn't likely to be acting like a normal person. He's not going to be rational. He'll probably do something stupid that will get all of you hurt…"

"We get lots of kids… They're your daytime burglars. They do it on the way home from school and when they should be out playing and studying. You can't help but feel sympathy for them because of their age. But, in many ways… they're well on their way to being hardened by life."

Arrive at the scene of an ongoing burglary at a commercial building or factory and it's like instant ulcers. You just can't size up the threat. You're apprehensive. You're a little scared. You anticipate the very worst, just to be on the safe side. You just know the thief isn't likely to be acting like a normal person. He's not going to be rational. He'll probably do something stupid that will get all of you hurt. I usually don't have any useful information about the guy beforehand other than that he's a thief and in the process of breaking into somebody's property. He may just shrug and give himself up, or he may be armed and willing to take me on if necessary.

In 1983 we responded to a burglary in a factory, and we chased two suspects from the top of a seven-floor building. We were checking floors, and I was in the basement. There were no lights there, and the two guys jumped me. I was lucky. I managed to beat them down and cuff them without using my gun. Fortunately, they didn't get me down first and take my pistol. I could have easily been hurt on that one. But eventually the two burglars were convicted and got two years apiece.

Another time a man broke into an apartment, but the owner had a German shepherd. The shepherd cornered him in the bedroom. He didn't attack him; he just kept the robber from fleeing. According to the apartment owner, the guy had broken in shortly after she'd left for work that morning. She didn't return home until about 10:30 that night. That's when she found this idiot lying on the bed. The whole day, he'd been pinned there, so scared his bodily functions had gone on him. That one has got to be the easiest pinch I've ever made!

In April of this year we got a radio call from a woman who'd been out in the backyard hanging clothes when she saw this guy slipping through the back door. When we arrived, we entered the house and made our way to the second floor, checking everything out and looking for the robber. We found him eventually. He'd hidden under a bed in the bedroom. He surrendered passively and didn't seem to

Peter Hendrie

Firing Range

Washington, D.C.

give a damn about losing his freedom. The guy didn't seem to be under the influence of anything, but I did notice he had track marks on his arms. My guess was he was on heroin, which would explain why he wasn't violent, just lackadaisical.

We had one fellow named Earl who started having serious problems when he was fourteen years old. He just kept getting locked up. It was like a revolving door with him. He first started dealing heroin at twelve. Within two years he was a user. That's when the car theft and the burglary started. Four or five nice kids used to hang out with him. I watched his influence on them — how they gradually changed from normal kids to messed-up ones like himself. Well, Earl's just gotten out of prison after doing ten year's hard time for being busted with a very, very large quantity of heroin. He no longer looks like the happy young lad; he wears the hard time on his face and in his movements. So far, I've had no trouble with Earl. Prison's sort of refined him. But it may just be that he's smarter now and won't get busted as easily anymore.

We don't see so many female burglars. But we get lots of kids, usually between the ages of fourteen and eighteen. They're your daytime burglars. They do it on the way home from school and when they should be out playing and studying. These youngsters have no respect for their parents or themselves, and they're certainly not going to work up any respect for us. You can't help but feel sympathy for them because of their age. But, in many ways, they're far older than their years, particularly in criminal outlook. They're well on their way to being hardened by life.

I've arrested kids as young as twelve years old for burglary. We nabbed one recently at a motorcycle shop. He was thirteen and was with his older brother and his friends. The kid was a willing participant. It wasn't like he was forced to do it. He just wanted to be one of the guys. The older boys stuffed him through a grate into the basement, and he handed stuff up to them. When we came along in the patrol car, the big ones ran, leaving the small kid in the basement until the owner arrived and let us in. The kid was still down in the cellar hiding behind the motorcycles. This was a very typical burglary. The peewee-sized kid is lifted through a window or some other small opening, and he hands the booty out to the others. The sad thing is that, going in, the small kid knows he is probably going to get caught. Most times, there's no easy way for him to get back out on his own. It's all a bit insane. These kids don't give a damn about their future or anything. They just don't seem to care.

We caught one such peewee and took him over to the juvenile division, where we contacted his mother. She was drunk at the time and couldn't come over right away. The first thing she did when she showed up was really beat on the kid. "Why did you get caught?" she yelled. She didn't say, "Why did you do this?" or "What do you think you're doing breaking the law?" just "How could you be so stupid to get caught?" So that was his role model. The kid probably hasn't had a chance since birth.

The vast majority of stolen goods are hustled on the streets in the neighborhood where they were lifted. The quickest way to sell something in this country is to say it's "hot." Doesn't matter to people whether it's stolen stuff or not — they jump for a bargain. It would sure make our work easier if people recorded serial numbers. Then we could help them out! Lots of people stencil and engrave their important possessions, but the thieves just say they put these IDs on themselves. But with serial numbers, once it's been recorded and you're in possession of the sales slip, that's undeniable evidence.

Most of the time the petty thief will sell the stuff on the street himself, unless he uses a fence who brokers it and sells to pawnshops and places like that. You get some guys who are entrepreneurs. They've got a few bucks, so they set themselves up to buy the stuff and get the word out in the neighborhood. They'll buy hot stuff and off-load it in a different city. We'll sometimes get info about these operations from citizens who come forward. But people aren't exactly tripping over each other to volunteer such help to the police. Usually they have to be motivated into doing it — they've been ripped off by some guy, or they don't think he's paying the right price for stolen goods. Naturally, these types never say they stole anything. It's always the husband or the brother that did it. But we get our information, nonetheless, and we proceed to get a warrant and lock up the budding entrepreneur.

I provide advice to small business owners on how to prevent a burglary whenever I can. Alarm systems seem to be in fashion, as do window grates and anything else that makes life more difficult for the burglar. If a place has had a problem in one area before, you should concentrate on securing that against burglars. Don't make yourself a target! Imagine how the burglar might enter your premises. Anticipate! Check out your plate-glass windows. In twentieth-century America now, the style is window grates. If you're not going to cover them, then take your merchandise out of the window at the end of each workday. Don't let your shop window be too attractive a prospect for some passing idiot. They're opportunists. If they see something glittering in your store, they'll readily smash the window to get their hands on it. You're not dealing with brain trusts here. If they were, they'd have jobs.

■

Most commercial burglar alarms go through police headquarters. We trace them and send out a call to officers who are nearest to the location. More than 90 percent of burglar alarms sounded are caused by technical malfunction or a careless employee accidentally tripping them rather than by a clumsy burglar.

It's impossible for us to tell which alarm is an accident and which is a real life burglar. We have to respond to them all. Perhaps more money could be put to designing a better alarm system, but in the interim maybe some ordinance should be passed fining people who keep tripping their own alarm systems. The problem is that the community doesn't realize the cost or the manpower it takes for us to respond to all these unfounded alarms. The public just thinks, "Well, that's the police officer's job." But when the cop's responding to false alarms, he's no longer on the beat protecting the community at large, and it's not like there are an infinite number of cops out there.

Responding to repeated unfounded alarms gets your guard down for when the real one occurs and there's a live, and potentially troublesome, burglar inside. They are a priority call, and we respond to them as quickly as we can. Imagine the frustration when you're taking these risks to get to a location fast and you know you've already rushed to the same address two or three times last week and four or five times during the past month. Each time it was a false alarm. You just have to keep practicing the techniques the academy taught to keep an edge and to remain alert for those situations when the burglar's really there.

Firing Range

Washington, D.C.

"All of our training is geared to the change on the streets. The narcotics dealers and traffickers we see out there are no longer afraid to take us on, and they've got the money and the means to purchase powerful weapons. Some are just kids, and they don't understand what death is all about, nor do they seem to care."

Carol Guzy (4)

40

You want to know who's a police officer's best partner? It's his weapon. He always knows what that partner's going to do — far more so than any rookie officer he might be teamed up with. It's the truth. I speak from twenty-one years experience as an officer and four as a firearm instructor.

It takes time for partners to really know each other's individual quirks and to learn to rely on each other. But with a weapon, as long as it's cared for, it won't run off or get cold feet. It'll stand by you, and you can tell it what to do. It's simply the best friend a police officer can have — on the street, under fire, and when you're in need of a partner to back you up.

I carried a thirty-eight for twenty-one years, but given the situation with crack and PCP and the violent nature of the people distributing it, we've changed weapons. If we're going to take on these people, we want to at least even the odds a bit. Now we use a nine-millimeter semiautomatic called the Glock 17 and 19. It has the highest firing capacity of any weapon currently on the market. An officer can be taught to put out a tremendous number of rounds in a very short period. With proper trigger control, he can also have a high degree of accuracy.

We did a survey of actual police shootings and discovered that out of every 100 rounds fired, only 18 hit their mark. The other 82 went wide and, given a police officer's luck, probably hit a parked Mercedes or a Cadillac or something else of value. The survey made us change our approach. Officers were no longer allowed to just hit anywhere on a silhouetted target. Their bullets had to land within the seven target rings. Then we told them 43 out of 50 shots had to hit, and we said you must shoot for a score and get 450 out of 600. That's a 75 percent accuracy rate. And we said if you shoot wildly all over the seven rings, you'd still fail, even though you got 75 percent. Our training is making them hit closer and closer to the bull's eye. And the results are showing! The accuracy of actual police shooting on the streets of Washington has now risen to 25 percent.

In the cabinet in the training division lobby is an honor roll with the badges of police officers killed in the line of duty. As firearm instructors, we are very close to these fallen comrades. Our responsibility is to instruct officers in a way that keeps them alive on the streets. Unfortunately, we have become increasingly convinced that in the past some of the badges ended up in that cabinet because the training was not as good as it could have been.

We convinced the powers that be at the training academy to let us change things a bit. We got new equipment and increasingly based training on actual street experience. Most of our permanent firearm instructors now have nineteen or twenty years of street savvy, and they still go back out on the street periodically to stay current. Our tactics have changed to reflect the kind of training the police officer out on the street actually says he needs.

Let's say some little old lady informs you her son is high on PCP in his bedroom only a few steps away. Suddenly he comes out and threatens the officer with a gun. We demonstrate how to turn and properly cover the target and avoid the "pray and spray" method, so that rather than just firing with the hope that you hit your target, you make sure you're missing any innocent bystanders.

Out on the target shooting range, we make you run and crouch and shoot from awkward positions. You fire at targets with innocent people in the way. You better be sure which is the real target, and you'd better be accurate.

In training officers, we go beyond basic marksmanship and teach tactics. We show them how to take on multiple targets and to shoot on the move and from automobiles and difficult positions. They learn to cover much more effectively than in the past.

All of our training is geared to the change on the streets. The narcotics dealers and traffickers we see out there are no longer afraid to take us on, and they've got the money and the means to purchase powerful weapons. Some are just kids, and they don't understand

" It takes time for partners to really know each other's individual quirks and to learn to rely on each other. But with a weapon, as long as it's cared for, it won't run off or get cold feet. It'll stand by you, and you can tell it what to do. It's simply the best friend a police officer can have."

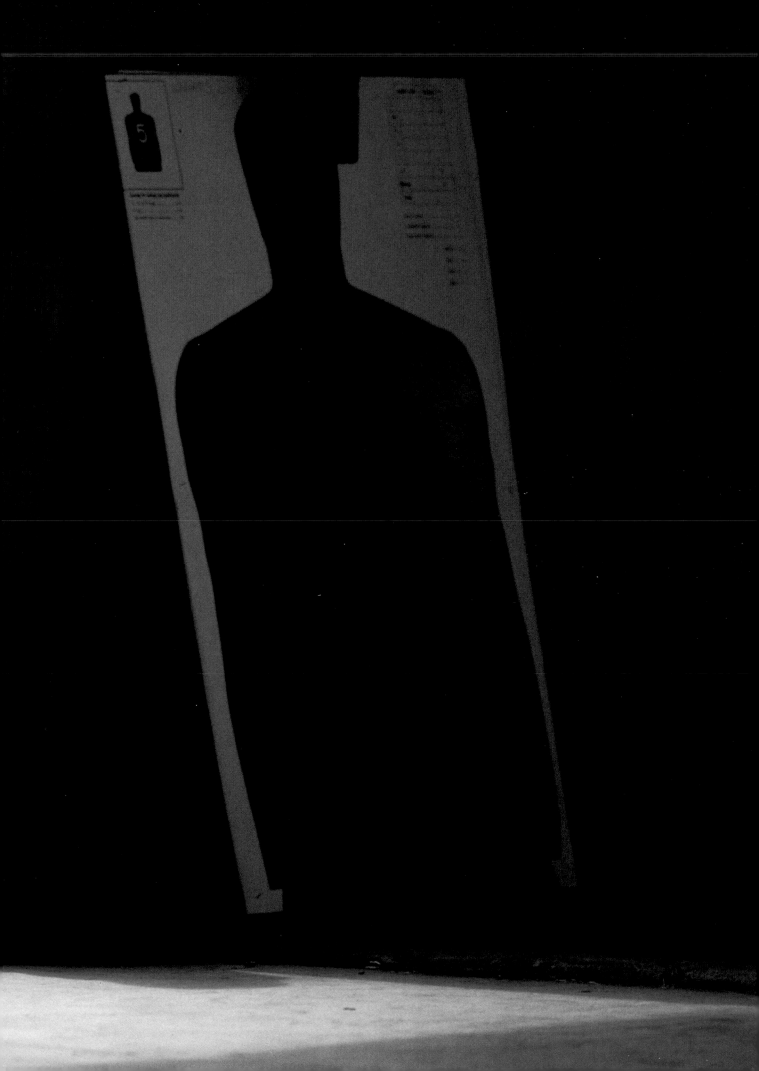

what death is all about, nor do they seem to care.

The officers themselves have put pressure on the hierarchy, saying, "Hey, it's time for us to change," if we're to meet the new threat on the streets. The department's responding, purchasing the kinds of training equipment that's needed, like pop-up targets, for instance.

Currently, we're trying to get a house to teach officers how to make "dynamic" entries and to rapidly search an apartment building, room by room, and seize narcotics. We aim to teach our officers to do it quickly, safely, and effectively, rather than the old hi-diddle-diddle way where they all knock on the door together and everybody rushes in at the same time. Try that against these new drug dealers, and all they'll do is shoot at the door and, bang, four or five cops are down. With the crisscross and buttonhook maneuvers we teach, officers get in and quickly clear the doorway and the room with just two officers. Using this technique they could clear an entire eight-room house in just thirty-two seconds!

Some of our officers are reluctant at first to learn new tricks. We had one detective from the Seventh District who didn't want to learn a new technique. In the car course, trainees open the vehicle door, lean out and shoot. Then they abandon the car for a protective barricade. At first this old veteran detective didn't want to listen to us or adopt the new technique. He just wanted to go through the motions and get back to his job on the street — narcotics.

Later he came back and said, "Larry, I want to apologize for giving you a rough time. I left here after the course, and I was in the street talking to a twelve-year-old kid about narcotic problems. Two automobiles pulled into the block, one a Mercedes. They got out and shot at this guy twice and beat the daylights out of him. Then they drove off. I followed. But they must have realized I was a police officer. One guy opened the car door on the passenger side and started to roll out on me. They would have had me dead in seconds.

"There I was in my car. About a car and a half away from them. They had me cold, and I didn't know what to do. Then I remembered the training. I slammed on the brake, moving the way you taught me. I swung open the door and braced myself and fired a few rounds. I didn't hit the guy, but one round went through the taillight, the back seat, the front seat, and slammed through the dashboard so hard it scared the hell out of the driver. He bailed out of the car, but I was on him like white on rice.

"The shooter, who I knew had the gun, because he used it earlier, took off running. He was scared because I came out of the car so fast. He wasn't about to take me on. He managed to flee, but I got the driver. His car just kept rolling and crashed over an embankment. We recovered money and all sorts of narcotics. We knew what these guys were up to. They were drug enforcers. They beat up and shot at the guy who was skimming money off the drugs he was selling for the organization. The enforcers were just giving him, and others like him, a warning."

When I first started teaching at the academy, I had an Officer Best as a trainee. The kid never drank or smoked. He was a vegetarian who worked out with weights. He was the wholesome American young man — never cussed, never raised his voice, never gave me a hard time, and graduated with good grades.

A year after Best graduated, he invited me to a class reunion to celebrate their first year as cops. That night he and his partner were chasing an auto theft suspect. His partner took off after one and Best took off after the other. Best simply ran around the corner. But the problem was that we had never taught how to round a corner properly. Nobody had ever taught him to do that. He lost his life at that moment, and I feel it was our fault. A lot of us instructors feel that we should have taught him something more about chasing people.

The courts already recognize this! They no longer ask, "When was the last time this officer qualified?" And you stipulate it was on such and such a date. Now they ask, "When was this officer last trained in weapon use, in identifying his target, and in shoot or no-shoot situations?"

I've seen real changes in the training program. Police officers stop by and say, "Larry, I want to thank you." One officer shook my hand, and I said, "What are you doing this for?" He responded, "Listen, I was in a shoot-out over the weekend. I was off duty at a service station getting gas when a car pulled up into a garage on Maryland Avenue. Gunfire erupted, and I confronted these guys coming out. I identified myself as a police officer, but they didn't stop."

This officer ended up taking on more than three subjects. We know he shot and disabled one of them. And we found blood trails from another one. All in all, forty-two rounds were fired at him. He came to me and said, "Larry, if I hadn't had that automatic — the weapon that you convinced the department to purchase — and if you hadn't taught me the zigzag and the use of cover courses, those guys would have surely killed me."

Most of my career has been spent in Washington's Third District, the smallest district within the metropolitan police department, but the one with the highest concentration of crime. I've worked narcotics and walked the street as a patrolman. Much of the training I received was through experience.

I recall one shoot-out incident where three of us were responding to a domestic disturbance on Eleventh Street. We were at the top of an extremely narrow stairwell. The apartment door suddenly burst open and a woman was thrown out, cut up and bleeding so bad she looked like a Thanksgiving turkey, and blood just splattered all over the wall. A man chased right after her with a butcher's knife.

We ordered him to drop the knife, but he was so enraged that he charged us. One officer hit him with his fist and another with a nightstick which, it was later revealed, broke his arm. After momentarily falling backward, the man charged again, knife still firmly in hand. At this point, we had no place to go and

no nightsticks or other defense except for our weapons. We opened up on him, and he went down.

You can tell yourself, well I'll do this and I'll do that after I shoot someone. But once you've actually done it, you live with quite an overwhelming feeling for a while, and you keep telling yourself that everything is okay, you did the best you possibly could.

In another incident, I was with a lieutenant investigating trouble on Tenth Street. He was at the front, another officer was behind him and I was at the bottom of the steps. The next thing I know, the other officer suddenly grabbed the lieutenant, kicked the door shut, and literally threw the lieutenant over the rail. When the door sprang open, I was looking up the barrel of a handgun. I did the old Vietnam zigzag. I mean, I hauled ass. I didn't know what the hell was going on. All I knew was that the first two officers had bailed out already.

We ended up inside with three people who were there to rob drug dealers. Under the cover of shotguns, we made arrests of the people there. You know, you can go your whole career and never have to draw your weapon or use it in vain. For some it can turn out like that.

Another incident involves the night sights we requested for the Glock which are good for about ten years. It doesn't really matter how dark it gets. If I can make out the shadow, I can hit the target. This is what happened. A young kid was running away from several police officers. The sergeant who told me about this incident arrived at the scene. He observed the kid running with a gun in his hand. The sergeant chased him into a dark parking lot area, and the kid kept running, but eventually slipped. He got up off the ground, and facing the sergeant, he raised his hands toward him. The sergeant wasn't sure if he still had the gun. He was sure, however, that he had it before running into the lot. He had seen it in the street light. But now it was so dark, all he could make out was the shadows.

Suddenly, the sergeant realized the kid did indeed have the gun. He brought his own up quickly, just like we teach officers to do. In tactical shooting, it's not so much lining up your front sight with the rear sight but shooting with your front sight and getting on target as quickly as possible. Extend it out at center mass with nice, smooth trigger control and hit your target. Eighty-seven percent of the time police shootings are five to ten feet away.

Those night sights are amazing. The sergeant saw his shadow, so he put the night sights on him, and he stuck out like a sore thumb. He fired a round and it struck him in the upper leg. The kid went down like a sack of potatoes. The sergeant recovered a .357 magnum from the kid, and it was clear he was trying to take him out. So even after a short period of time, we know our tactics, and these Glocks combined with the night sights are saving police officers.

In the future, even more radical tactics and weapons are going to be needed. Unless society changes its mind about how people treat each other, you are never going to get the gun out of the police officer's hand. DNA identification is one heck of a breakthrough, as radical a change as when they discovered fingerprinting. But the changes in terms of revolvers and firearms training is on the move to better, more reliable, and more rapid-firing handguns. They're experimenting with a ten-millimeter right now. It's still too bulky and heavy and not very reliable, but if it's ever developed, it'll have some real knockdown power.

Even though our weapons are getting better, we exhaust every means prior to resorting to using firearms for fear of endangering an innocent bystander. It's department guidelines, and we teach it to our officers. Even if you're scared, you've got to be thinking about what are reasonable grounds, reasonable causes, and reasonable proof to use your weapon. Twenty years ago, if a guy was standing in front of you threatening to kill you with a baseball bat, you'd probably shoot him rather than take him on. A baseball bat can do a lot of damage, especially in the hands of a strong individual. But today you probably wouldn't fire unless the individual made a move to actually do harm.

Now, in every district, we have a Taser unit that sends out fifty thousand volts of electricity. We'll use equipment like this to incapacitate the person before resorting to firearms. Or we might use Mace, or even our barricade units. They talk to you, soothing emotions, waiting you out, before turning to force. But should we ever need to use firearms on you, we want to do it with the least amount of danger to you or innocent bystanders.

We don't just use firearms for the hell of it, just to see what they do. Hopefully, people realize that we have to live with the consequences and that we're not superheroes with S's on our chests. Police officers are human beings too. We have families and responsibilities to go home to at night. We have small children who are waiting for us at the door.

You know, it must be nice to be a city administrator or mayor and tell your voters you've got a two-hundred-million-dollar surplus in the budget, so reelect me. But if you got that surplus by skimping on your budget for police training, you've done a disservice to your officers and to the community as a whole. Train your officers well, give them the proper equipment, and they will get the job done. And when the action starts, a cop is going to do what he is trained to do. Instinct takes over. The spirit of our training task is written in our motto above the door, "Your survival is our concern."

"You can tell yourself, well I'll do this and I'll do that after I shoot someone.
But once you've actually done it, you live with quite an overwhelming feeling for a while, and you keep
telling yourself that everything is okay, you did the best you possibly could."

Shoplifting

Cincinnati, Ohio

"Generally, shoplifting isn't a violent crime. It's a secretive one. By nature, shoplifters don't want to be seen. They're sneak-type thieves. But the drug addict is different. He's the truly dangerous thief. He can be stealing a three-dollar item like cough syrup, which many of them are into, and he's packing a .357 magnum in his pocket."

W e get all kinds of shoplifters downtown. And some of them can be pretty funny. Last week I went over to a store where they'd apprehended a guy leaving with eighteen pairs of jeans. They first detected him gathering jeans in the men's department. He tried to exit through the bakery shop but got caught. He was just carrying them out, real casual, not really concealing them, hoping nobody would spot him. He even had a friend in a car across the street waiting for him. I don't think he had any use for eighteen pairs of jeans. He was probably going to sell them. Most people steal one or two items, things they can use.

Shoplifters aren't all that ingenious. They usually get caught sooner or later. Most aren't really that smart. They'll carry an empty duffel bag to drop the merchandise into or go into the dressing rooms and put on the clothes they're planning to steal.

Nevertheless, it's a pretty serious crime, and it adds up. Each year the department stores lose a phenomenal amount of merchandise. And the consumers end up footing the bill in higher prices. In Ohio, estimates show that shoplifting costs each family about $200 a year in price increases.

Downtown is my beat. It's mostly stores and retail businesses. I'll normally see at least one shoplifter a day. The major chain stores get lots of them. They have large security staffs that are well trained and keep photos of the regular shoplifters and the professionals. When they arrest a shoplifter, they do most of the paperwork, and everything's ready when we get to the store. We just look the place over and take the prisoner and the paperwork over to the justice center for processing. In most stores an employee or the manager detains the suspect. We then write it up and take the store employee along with us to file a complaint. In these instances our job is basically paperwork and transporting the prisoner.

In the inner-city stores, you get a lot of grocery and drugstore shoplifting. Especially during the Christmas and holiday seasons. In the big department stores, it's mainly clothing.

"We're seeing the same faces, the same shoplifters, over and over again. A guy doesn't usually get caught shoplifting and then say, "Oh, that's the end of my shoplifting career!" We're talking about repeat offenders. If they just get court citations or small fines, so what? They live by shoplifting. The occasional arrest and fine just come with the job."

A lot of kids seem to take to shoplifting. It's almost a fad with them. After school, they'll take a bus downtown, go into the stores, and grab whatever they can. We also get the impulsive shoplifters, like the sixty-three-year-old lady who attempted to steal twelve boxes of garbage bags which I'm sure she didn't need. She had more than seventy-five dollars on her, but she stashed the goods in her bag and walked out without paying. She had no previous record of shoplifting. The store opted for the humane solution. They let her pay for the bags and leave.

■

Shoplifting is a crime that's committed by all ages and all ethnic and economic groups. There's no group that doesn't shoplift. Naturally your drug addicts, who have to feed a three-hundred-dollar-a-day habit, will tend to do it more. And some of the poor and unemployed, who have no other source of income, sometimes make it a career. But you'll also find rich businessmen doing it for the thrill of stealing. Even decent people who suddenly are confronted with an opportunity grab things, sometimes of little value. They just go for it on impulse. The professional shoplifters are actually trained. They're taught to wear harnesses under their dresses or business suits to conceal the stuff they steal. And they're sent out to city and suburban stores to practice shoplifting.

Your serious shoplifters are also sustaining major fencing operations. The shoplifters will unload merchandise for 10 to 25 percent of its value. A junkie may settle for next to nothing for his stuff, so he has to shoplift an enormous amount just to keep going. We even had one fencing operation in the city where no money changed hands at all. Drugs were given to the shoplifters in exchange for the goods they stole.

It's going to be next to impossible to curb all the shoplifting in downtown stores. So many people are doing it! But a local department store has a limited budget and can afford only so many security measures. With

"There's no group that doesn't shoplift... Some of the poor and unemployed, who have no other source of income, sometimes make it a career. But you'll also find rich businessmen doing it for the thrill of stealing. Even decent people who suddenly are confronted with an opportunity grab things, sometimes of little value."

hundreds and thousands of people walking the aisles, they can only watch so many. The percentage caught is probably very, very small.

Store security can always be improved with better lighting and more open display areas. More expensive clothing can be tagged electronically with beepers that go off at the door. And there can always be better training. Even more video cameras and surveillance technology could be used. A lot of stores are already using this gear on a limited basis.

A police force can only respond to a shoplifting incident once it occurs. The store's security staff does most of the actual surveillance and detecting. However, some policemen will moonlight, providing security in these stores once they're off duty.

Generally, shoplifting isn't a violent crime. It's a secretive one. By nature, shoplifters don't want to be seen. They're sneak-type thieves. But the drug addict is different. He's the truly dangerous thief. He can be stealing a three-dollar item like cough syrup, which many of them are into, and he's packing a .357 magnum in his pocket. Store security or the police confront him, and it can quickly escalate into a deadly confrontation. A friend of mine was recently bitten severely in the arm and injured fighting a shoplifter. In the AIDS era, this kind of thing is a real concern for police officers.

In fact, we now carry a powerful disinfectant in our patrol cars that will kill the AIDS virus externally. But if you get it internally, there's no cure. When we stop a shoplifter or any other suspect, we're careful handling the razors or needles he might have in his pockets. Before, we just grabbed. Now we use rubber gloves to search, and when in contact with the body fluids of a victim or a prisoner.

If it was my choice, I'd set some stiffer penalties for shoplifters. Sentences would be automatic. And I'm a firm believer in publicizing criminals, so I'd put their names and faces in the newspaper for everyone to see! This would probably stop the neighborhood housewife or the kid from dropping an item

in their pockets. Putting every shoplifter in jail for thirty days is a nice idea as well, but we don't have room. We literally don't have the space! Our jails would be full of shoplifters in no time at all.

My approach may sound a little hard but we're seeing the same faces, the same shoplifters, over and over again. A guy doesn't usually get caught shoplifting and then say, "Oh, that's the end of my shoplifting career!" We're talking about repeat offenders. If they just get court citations or small fines, so what? They live by shoplifting. The occasional arrest and fine just come with the job.

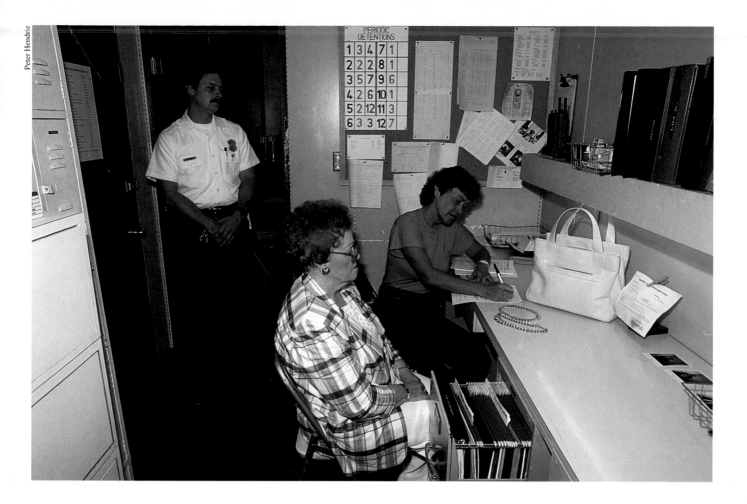

Peter Hendrie

"A lot of kids seem to take to shoplifting. It's almost a fad with them. After school, they'll take a bus downtown, go into the stores, and grab whatever they can. We also get the impulsive shoplifters, like the sixty-three-year-old lady who attempted to steal twelve boxes of garbage bags which I'm sure she didn't need."

School Patrol

Chicago, Illinois

"We like to think of schools as special places where only learning occurs. It's not true! Our schools are miniversions of the interaction that exists in the neighborhoods around them. So if you've got crime in your community, the chances are good that it'll spill over into your schools."

If you've got a problem with drugs or gang activity in the community, then don't be surprised to find it in the schools as well. We like to think of schools as special places where only learning occurs. It's not true! Our schools are mini-versions of the interaction that exists in the neighborhoods around them. So if you've got crime in your community, the chances are good that it'll spill over into your schools.

Our job is to keep a lid on crime and make sure it doesn't get out of control. Over the past few years, we've been very involved in helping to designate schoolgrounds as safe havens so that the bad stuff happening in the community doesn't have the chance to creep into the classroom. We've attempted to do that by education, legislation, and by checking IDs of kids as they come to school to screen out any that don't belong. We've also helped get passage of a safe-school-zone ordinance. That ordinance makes a crime, like selling drugs, for example, a much more serious offense if it's done in or around the school.

We maintain a strong presence in the schools. Our investigators check out crimes committed by and against juveniles, and our school patrol force, consisting of one hundred twenty-nine uniformed police officers, has classrooms, playing fields, and the general area around schools as its beat. We also have two-person cars that respond to incidents in the forty-five schools that don't have police officers assigned full time.

Crime in Chicago schools is a reflection of society in general, and I don't consider things out of control. I may be biased, but I think we've done a good job targeting school-related criminal activity and attacking the problem. We do have our incidents, however. One of the worst was when a deranged man shot two people in an auto parts store across the street from the school. He then left the store, walked over to the school building, and shot a janitor and a garbage collector. Two of my school officers happened to be there at an unrelated incident. They encountered the gunman in the school building, and he ended up shooting and killing our female officer, and

"School officers are specially chosen for their jobs. They can relate to kids and work well around the school. You can't put just any police officer in there. It's got to be a cop whose primary goal is to help and guide youngsters, not arrest them."

wounding her male partner in both legs. He in turn returned fire and killed the gunman. Our losses were great, but we were also fortunate. Had our officers not encountered the man, we might have seen a repeat of last year's gruesome spectacle in which a woman walked into a suburban classroom, and shot a number of children.

We've increased our school patrols in recent years, mainly to relieve some of the pressure on the district police stations. If our school officers don't respond to calls in the schools, then a district officer would have to. That takes him away from his normal service calls. It's no good for anyone if someone's being robbed and assaulted in the street, but the police officer is tied up responding to a school call.

Truancy is a big problem. If the kid's not at school, he may be out there committing a crime or possibly becoming a victim himself. We've stepped up truancy prevention to stop just such crimes. We have truancy vans that go around looking for these kids, picking them up and returning them to their schools. We've even managed to uncover a variety of criminal activities that involve students as a result of this program. It's a fairly unique program and we're one of the few large city departments that have it. We also have a role-model program in which we get successful people, preferably those who've graduated from that particular school, to talk with the kids about their lives and careers.

One program I'd like to see here works well in keeping kids in the classroom in several big city schools around the country. Students are told they won't be able to take driver's education and get that precious driver's license unless their general classroom attendance record is good. The Board of Education runs the school's driver education program in Chicago, so it should be fairly easy to get such a program operating. I'm all for it!

Some people have referred to today's school kids as "the lost generation." I'm pretty sensitive to that. As a society, we've an obligation to ensure our kids are well educated. It's a kind of investment for the future.

The desire to provide them a good learning experience cuts across all economic and racial lines. Society wants it! If the chance to be educated is going to be interrupted by criminal activity — either by or against students — I take it very seriously. I'd like to reverse that attitude of people thinking of our kids as lost. If we call them lost, we're equally lost as a society. And we should be held as strictly responsible as they are. I'm accountable as far as law enforcement goes. The Board of Education has its responsibilities and the courts have theirs. But I can't overemphasize how important it is to have us all working together — police, Board of Ed, and the courts — rather than each going off on its own. It just has to be a concerted effort!

■

I have a good relationship with most students. I'm responsible for forty-seven schools, and I have a different relationship with all the kids. With a few of them, it doesn't matter what you do, you can't reach them. But the majority of them are good kids. They're just a lot of different personalities. You just feel your way through, guided by the way the kid talks, acts, and looks. It's always come easy for me to relate to kids.

A few years ago we had an incident in which a student was disgruntled, didn't like his teacher. They had had personality clashes. One day the student came into the school and tried to lure the teacher out of his classroom and into the hallway. After a while the kid made enough noise that the teacher came out. Well, the youngster had a gun and opened fire on the teacher, attempting to kill him. He missed, though, and fled out of the school. We arrested him on the street a while later. He didn't resist or anything.

There are gangs, and then there are gangs in Chicago. We've got a lot of teenagers here who call themselves gang members, but they're really not. They just long for something or someone to identify with. They'll tell you they're members of the Vice-Lords or the Disciples or whatever, but usually they don't know who the gang leader is, and they don't really answer to anybody. I consider them renegades, although renegades that can cause a lot of trouble and hurt people.

Most of the gangs use hand signals that our officers now know. Years ago, when they first started it, the hand signals were secret. Now they're much more open. The gang members wear different-colored hats, pitched on their heads in specific ways. Everything's special — their socks, their shoelaces, and their gold rings. It's like plumage, there are so many separate identifications.

I get considerable satisfaction from working in the schools. When I first came to this unit eight years ago, the gangs were growing rapidly and the crime rate was higher. Gang activity may have dropped over the years because kids are getting brighter. They're better educated, and they say, sure, it's nice to be a gang-banger, but it doesn't really get me anywhere. Some of the younger kids have actually seen their sisters, brothers and cousins shot and buried for no reason at all. They're growing up smarter. The more the police can help these kids come to the conclusion that gangs are a dead-end street, the better. Ninety percent of the students will come to this understanding on their own. But the rest won't. These are the ones that cause the problems, but we keep on trying!

■

Gangs and narcotics have been, without a doubt, my major headache in my years on the force. We've got gangs coming in from all different areas of town. They've got different identifying signs and wear their special outfits and caps. Naturally there's friction between the gangs, and it leads to fights. Our police officers are familiar with all these groups and their different members, so they keep fights to a minimum and control the situation. But there's no way a police officer can control it a hundred percent, because up to three thousand kids are in one school. Four or five gangs are operating in a single school alone. It's an impossible situation! There's no way one police

"A police officer in a school is doing what twenty cops would normally do in a district of equivalent size. If a robbery occurs or if a teacher gets assaulted or something gets stolen from a car, the school officer makes the investigation. The police officer has to serve in every law enforcement capacity at the school."

officer can control that, but at least the officers minimize the problem.

As well as controlling gangs, we deal with thefts and make arrests if we have evidence on someone. If battery is committed in a fight, we'll detain the person doing the assaulting. Our officers patrol all around the school to prevent such activity. Our truancy program was instituted some years ago, and takes action against those kids who hang out around a school though they don't attend it. The officer will write up a school laxity form and notify the other school that this student is in the wrong place so that appropriate action can be taken.

Some schools don't even have a police officer, though we've recommended they be assigned them. If we had extra cops, I'm sure the schools would function better and we'd be able to police some of the unseen criminal activity that's inevitable in a student body of thousands. A police officer in a school is doing what twenty cops would normally do in a district of equivalent size. If a robbery occurs or if a teacher gets assaulted or something gets stolen from a car, the school officer makes the investigation. The police officer has to serve in every law enforcement capacity at the school.

If a police officer makes an arrest, he usually has a meeting with the parents. He does this even in those incidents that may not have led to an arrest but were serious nonetheless. You know, we can't make an arrest for every petty thing or we'd be overwhelmed. But at least getting the parents in for a chat achieves something. It gets them directly involved, along with us, in their child's problem.

Kids commit every kind of crime. We have thefts from lockers, major batteries and assaults, robberies where students mug each other, and all the gang-related crime and the intimidation and threats that go along with it.

School officers are specially chosen for their jobs. They can relate to kids and work well around the school. You can't put just any police officer in there. It's got to be a cop whose primary goal is to help and guide youngsters, not arrest them. And in many ways he's a model for the kind of person kids may want to be when they're older.

■

Our officers went out to pick up a kid from school on charges of aggravated assault. Armed with a search warrant, we entered his home and found a closet cache of firearms. He had everything from zip guns to sophisticated weaponry, and he'd obviously been taking target practice — testing the weapons by firing them into the closet wall. It looked like World War III had taken place in there. Thank God the wall was thick enough, because it faced the stairwell and he could have easily seriously injured a neighbor. When I asked the kid's mom if she was aware that he was stockpiling weapons, she claimed total ignorance! It was unbelievable.

Our youth division benefits the whole community. We've managed to form strong links with school principals and even with some of the kids. It's a relationship that develops over time. We're amongst the U.S. leaders in programs that combat child exploitation. And we're particularly sensitive to a child's special needs in such circumstances. We do everything possible to limit the potential for further psychological scarring in the aftermath of abuse. We take a pro-active stance in arresting sexual and physical abuse offenders and concentrate on multiple offender cases.

One thing always leads to another in this field. For instance, recently we checked out a truancy case. A girlfriend had confessed in tears to us that her friend had been hanging out at a place just a couple of blocks from the school. When we went there, we discovered it was an abandoned house that had been set up as headquarters for one of the gangs that operates in the vicinity of the school.

This gang was enticing school kids into all kinds of sexual and drug activity and who knows what else. We were lucky, this time. We were able to clean 'em out of their hangout. But only temporarily. Schoolgrounds are prime recruiting areas for gangs and all that activity. They'll just spring up again.

Drug Interception

Fort Lauderdale, Florida

"The profile of the user is just about everybody. Go into the hottest night-clubs in Fort Lauderdale, Miami, and Palm Beach. They're full of drugs… more drug transactions take place than drinks are ordered. You know, I don't work twenty-four hours a day to risk my wife getting hit by some guy in a brand new BMW with his face full of white powder."

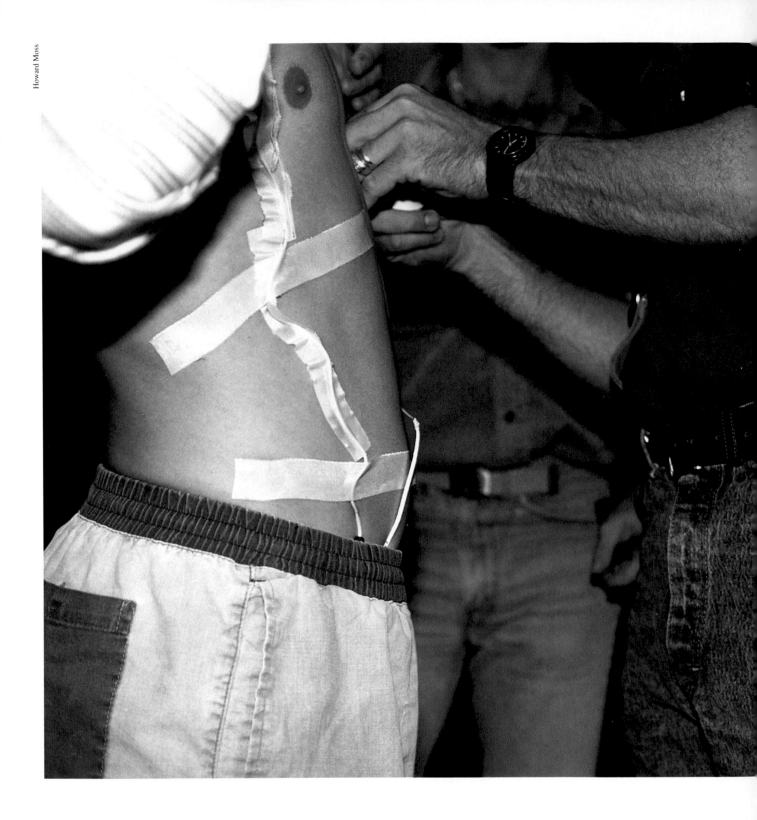

"*I'm no Don Quixote or Roger Rabbit. And I really take exception to*
filmmakers who try to make criminals look like Warren Beatty and Faye Dunaway in Bonnie and Clyde.
These drug smugglers are crooks, and they belong in one place, and that's jail."

Get the drug dealers off the streets — that's our objective. Another unit hooks the big fish who are buying large quantities of drugs. And a third one targets the wholesale shipments of cocaine and marijuana that are entering South Florida.

The police department and the city are now fully committed to making a dent in drugs. We have plans to beef up the force with up to seventy officers in the next several years. But this thing's an epidemic! There are close to two hundred locations in this city that are active distribution points for crack cocaine.

Marijuana used to be big, but now it's crack cocaine. That's the drug of choice in Fort Lauderdale. It's cheap, and it's an intense high. Our officers are getting burned out fast just chasing the stuff. Whether they're investigating larcenies, armed robberies, or muggings — they all come up with crack cocaine. Talk to the detectives about their arrests. Eight times out of ten these people have crack cocaine habits. Ninety-nine percent of the street prostitutes have crack cocaine habits. Often domestic disturbances are drug-related with people high on crack.

Most of the crack in this city gets "stepped on," with additional ingredients being added to dilute it. This increases the rocks, and the money they're going to make selling it. It's very easy: boil water with baking powder and add the powder cocaine. But before the powder cocaine is added, dump in other worthless stuff to stretch it.

Out on the street, we're dealing with felons, and it's not unusual to encounter somebody with a weapon. We're always cautious and take enough officers to stop the suspect if he runs or flees in a vehicle. And we never let ourselves get outnumbered. We're well trained with our own weapons, though we seldom actually use them. An officer in this unit has probably fired his weapon once in the last year. That's low, when you consider the numbers of guns we're taking off the street.

You have to laugh sometimes at things on the street. Today we arrested a girl with about a hundred dollars and some gold jew-

elry. She wanted it back! But it was money she got illegally from selling crack cocaine. She actually thought she was entitled to it. Some of them are so blasé about it. Getting arrested is as normal as getting up in the morning. They go to jail for a couple of days, and then it's back on the street.

I'm not sure we're getting the degree of cooperation from the justice system that's deserved. They want us to make an impact on a very severe problem, but we don't get their support. We make arrests, but these people do so little time in jail. We've got to nail a person two or three times for selling crack cocaine before the courts will give them any serious time.

If we could get some cooperation from the courts and really educate the kids — give them better role models than the fourteen-, fifteen-, eighteen- and twenty-year-olds they see dealing crack — then we'd see some success in dealing with the drug problem.

■

We had this one investigation in which a male dope-dealer and several hookers had set up house. Through surveillance I noticed that the prostitutes were bringing guys in and doing drugs. I managed to buy drugs there myself several times. I got real friendly with them. Finally, one day the boss was there, so we broke down the door and arrested the lot of them. The great part of the story is that when we emerged from the house, the entire block was standing there applauding us. What a feeling! They gave us drinks and desserts. They wrote thank-you cards. They said we were the best guys in the world.

After the bust we turned the tables. We sat in the house and pretended we were drug dealers. Even brought in our own drugs. When the customers came buying, we busted 'em. We were in business all night long!

Another time, a Jamaican drug dealer was working the city. We'd arrested him numerous times for weapon and cocaine violations, but we just couldn't keep him off the streets. This guy was truly disgusting! He'd

make prostitutes perform all kinds of kinky sex acts for drugs. One poor man needed drugs so bad that he forced his wife to have sex with the Jamaican, right in front of him. All for twenty dollars in cocaine! We heard these stories again and again. It was offensive, so we decided to really work on this guy. We nailed him on eight or nine felony counts, and he ended up doing time here before being deported to a Jamaican jail.

The Jamaican dealers in this area can be particularly vicious. They're violent and love automatic weapons. And they won't hesitate to use them. They'll spray an entire crowd with gunfire, just to get one guy.

In one incident an undercover agent entered a Jamaican house to buy three thousand dollars worth of crack cocaine. After he was in, they slammed the door on him. He was in a bad spot, and for a few minutes they terrorized him and threatened to kill him. They stole his gold jewelry and his wallet and even got the gun he had in his waistband. He was absolutely sure he was going to die.

The officer was wired with a body bug, and the police unit outside responded. One of the Jamaicans saw the police coming, but by then they had found the undercover cop's badge in his wallet, and they were on the run. They fled out the back door, but we caught them. Luckily, we came out on top in this one, but it could have easily gone the other way. Such are the dangers undercover officers face.

■

The boats are not like the streets. Things are a little more complacent. Drug interdiction is really secondary. When we do boat intercepts and go after drug traffickers, it's usually in major operations with customs or the Coast Guard.

The small boat smuggler is almost a thing of the past on this coast because so many law enforcement agencies are active. But some smugglers are certainly ingenious. One fifty-one-foot sailboat sailed to Europe and in North Africa was completely gutted. The boat's interior was lined with hashish, and

then it was repaneled and sailed back to the States. Once we discovered it, the chain saws and drills went to work. By the time we had finished searching, the boat was an empty shell, scrap wood.

There's nothing glamorous about going after water smugglers. I'm no Don Quixote or Roger Rabbit. And I really take exception to filmmakers who try to make criminals look like Warren Beatty and Faye Dunaway in *Bonnie and Clyde*. People come away thinking they're just wonderful. These drug smugglers are crooks, and they belong in one place, and that's jail.

The drug situation is worse than it's ever been, and I don't see a stop to it unless the government convinces the producer countries that it's not in their economic interest to grow the stuff. Countries like Peru, Bolivia, Colombia. Land that was once cultivated for coffee is now cultivated for coca plants. That television commercial with Juan Valdez picking coffee beans! That's a joke. Why should he pick coffee beans for ten cents a day when he can pick coca leaves and make ten bucks a day?

Research needs to be done on the reasons people take drugs in the first place. The poor ones do it to escape. A guy is on the job fifteen hours a day, six days a week and comes home to a hot, pest-infested apartment that he can barely afford. He escapes through drugs or alcohol. But people who are supposedly educated and have a degree — I don't understand them at all. It may be the in thing, but that's no excuse.

A lot of people think drug problems are

"A guy is on the job fifteen hours a day, six days a week and comes home to a hot, pest-infested apartment that he can barely afford. He escapes through drugs or alcohol. But people who are supposedly educated and have a degree — I don't understand them at all. It may be the in thing, but that's no excuse."

only in the major metropolitan areas. I've traveled to remote places with one traffic light, and there are drugs everywhere. Just ask a kid and he'll tell you where to go for that drug of your choice.

It's practically a culture. Here on the water, we stop people and they're very laid back about it. "Well, hell, man, I took my best shot and I got caught. I want my lawyer to work it out."

One individual I know started out unloading bales for a smuggler. He made enough money to buy a boat and contracted to haul loads for others. Then he started hauling for himself until, eventually, he could afford to buy an eighty-foot motor yacht to haul his loads. The thing was worth about three million dollars. When that vessel was seized, the guy just shook his head and said, "So what? That's the cost of doing business." He went off to see the wizard and did seven years in jail, which is a long time for a doper. He's probably back in business already, wearing the gold chains and with the big boats. I don't care how frugal your lifestyle is, you don't make that kind of money as a salesman.

As for the dealers, I don't want to point the finger at any one group. It used to be your white Anglo-Saxon that was doing it. Now there are a lot of Cubans, Haitians, and Jamaicans dealing on the street level. Any guy who wants to make a buck and is too lazy to work, he's the guy who's into it.

The profile of the user is just about everybody. Go into the hottest nightclubs in Fort Lauderdale, Miami, and Palm Beach. They're full of drugs. There are a couple of waterfront places in Fort Lauderdale where more drug transactions take place than drinks are ordered. You know, I don't work twenty-four hours a day to risk my wife getting hit by some guy in a brand new BMW with his face full of white powder. That's one of the things I think about.

Arrest Warrants

Louisville, Kentucky

"There's always an element of danger involved in serving a warrant. You're taking someone's freedom away from them. And if the man or woman has relatives, they often come to the person's aid. We have to fight them off, and officers sometimes get hurt."

W e're like the postman who delivers a special delivery letter except we usually bring bad news: "You're going to jail!" When a serious offender hasn't shown up at a court hearing on his case, the court issues a felony warrant. We're the guys who go out and serve them on the criminals. Any peace officer in the state of Kentucky can do it.

There's always an element of danger involved in serving a warrant. You're taking someone's freedom away from them. That's a threat to them. And if the man or woman has relatives, they often come to the person's aid. We have to fight them off, and officers sometimes get hurt in these scuffles.

Usually only one of us goes to serve a warrant. Each car carries the warrants for his particular patrol area. If we have a suspect we don't know, or if we think he might be armed, we'll call another car and have a backup unit waiting. It's all based on the nature of the crime and what we know about the particular suspect. Sometimes, though, given the time of day, we won't have an additional unit available when it's needed.

If the suspect is employed, we try to catch him when he comes home from work or before he leaves. I don't like to arrest somebody at work unless it is a very serious felony warrant, because it looks bad. We pick things up from experience. For example, if you know the guy's what we call a rabbit — he's likely to run — then we send an officer around back to block his exit. It's nice to knock on the door and then watch him run right into the officer's arms. Very satisfying. If he's in somebody else's house and only his address is on the warrant, then you can't enter the house he's in. You'll need a search warrant, unless the person who owns the house lets you in.

Repeat offenders have been through the process of getting arrested so many times that they normally aren't violent. They just try to take flight to avoid the whole thing. Sometimes the chases are something else. Fortunately, some of the younger officers can run a little faster than us old ones. Lots of times we're just playing hide-and-seek. They get up

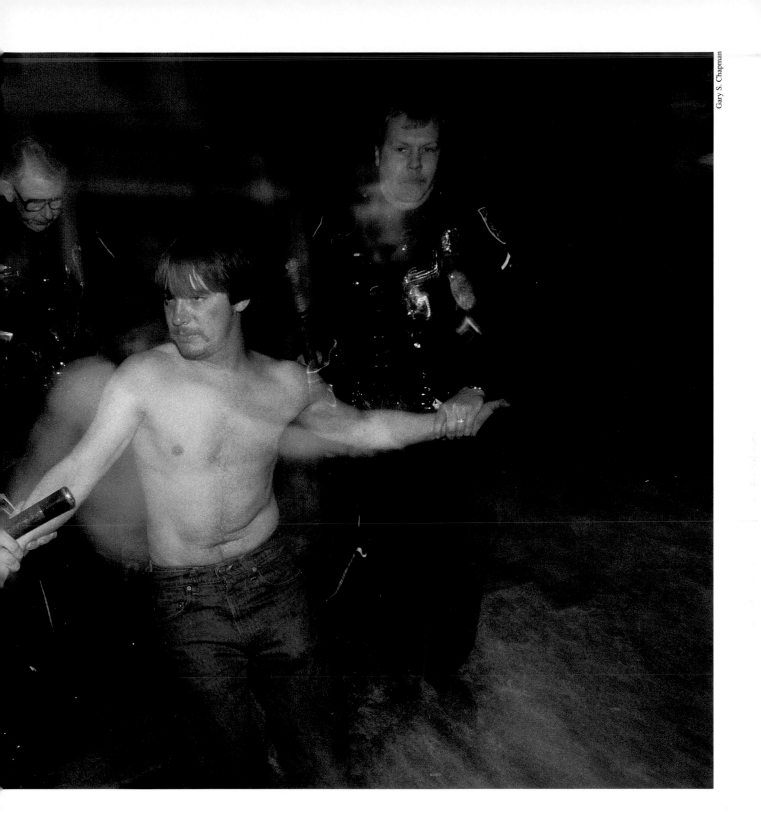

Gary S. Chapman

" If the suspect is employed, we try to catch him when he comes home from work or before he leaves. If you know the guy's what we call a rabbit — he's likely to run — then we send an officer around back to block his exit. It's nice to knock on the door and then watch him run right into the officer's arms. Very satisfying."

in attics, in between the rafters, and in basements, under piles of dirty clothes, and in between mattresses, anything to keep their freedom.

The general reaction when we show up to serve a warrant is both shock and anger. When they're mad, you have to be extra careful. But some people are real easy about it. They'll say, "Well, I've been waiting for you guys to get here. What took you so long?" It depends on the type of person you're dealing with. If he's Joe-everyday-worker, he'll get mad. "You're kidding? They took a warrant out on me? They have no right!" Or sometimes they act like they don't believe you and say, "That's impossible. That thing's no good. It couldn't be." Lots of times the offenders know there are warrants out on them and they do their best to avoid being caught. We often have to use a little trickery to get them. We try not to serve warrants on Christmas Day — that's a bit rough — but Sunday morning is a good time. You catch them off guard, and they just calmly answer the door. Sunday morning, that's when you can really surprise 'em!

After a while you serve so many warrants that it's second nature. You think nothing's going to happen. That's a big mistake. If you just walk up and stand in front of the door, taking no precautions, you're going to get hurt sooner or later. You just can't allow yourself to get lazy. I've found you tend to be more careful if you're alone and drive by yourself. With a partner, you lax up a bit.

When we go into a house on a warrant arrest, we'll usually call on the radio that we're off on a 1085 — that's code for a wanted person. We'll just let them know where we are; for example, "We're at such and such an address, and are out of the car on a 1085."

One time we had a robbery warrant down in a housing project. The lady swore that the guy we were after wasn't there, but we had received information that he was. We looked all over but couldn't find him. One of the officers walked through the house a couple of times, and even though we had a warrant, the woman was raising all kinds of hell about our being there. Eventually, one of the guys sat down on the bed. Guess what? It moved. Turns out the man had sandwiched himself between the mattress and the box springs. If that one cop hadn't sat down on the job, we'd never have gotten the guy!

Another time we forced our way into an apartment, and a woman swore the man we were looking for wasn't around. Turns out she was right. He wasn't. The guy actually lived in the apartment next door. We'd made a big mistake, and it was a bit embarrassing. The city ended up paying for the damage. Stuff like that happens from time to time.

Many people use warrants to resolve domestic trouble. A guy's been living with his girl, and then he takes up with some other woman. The first girl takes out a warrant on him. It's a club she can use against him. Usually these are misdemeanor, not felony, warrants, but we serve both. I don't particularly like many of these warrants, and I don't like serving them. They stem from domestic trouble, and often they're shaky. Seems to me there must be a better way to deal with these people and their domestic problems other than serving them a warrant and dragging them in.

Street Narcotics

Kansas City, Missouri

"In the past I've thought, 'Gosh, it can't get much worse than this.' That was when I was in narcotics and PCP was on the rampage. Then there were these laced marijuana cigarettes that created instant psychos. That was wild, and I thought, 'This has got to be the worst!' But then along comes crack, and 'worst' is redefined! It's not only truly bad, but it's everywhere."

Any time you're out buying drugs from the dealers, the adrenaline gets popping. You don't really know who these people are that you're about to contact. You don't know what's about to happen. You've made so many arrests in the past that you live in fear that you're going to be recognized by some guy as the cop who busted him for carrying a weapon or whatever.

Even with all this anxiety, I keep myself going by knowing that I'm actually doing something to rid society of the drug epidemic. I have the self-satisfaction of knowing I'm doing some good.

One time, while I was undercover on a drug purchase, I entered a room and immediately recognized most of the bad guys in there as people I'd arrested in the past when I was a uniformed cop. They were robbers and burglars who had been charged with major crimes against people. I did my deal, and they didn't even recognize me. When I went back again later, it was easier; I was more confident. I knew what I was up against, and in my mind I was chuckling, knowing that now I can put these guys away for a long, long time.

That gives me a lot of satisfaction, because I get them off the street for several years and they won't be hurting anybody. The drug dealers are society's piranhas. They have no morals. They're just greedy people who contribute nothing to society and care about nothing but themselves and their drug profits.

When you're dealing with drug dealers, you have to let your confidence come out. You gotta act like you're one of them, that you're hooked on drugs or you're getting 'em for your wife or girlfriend or for some Joe Blow down the street.

One time we hit a house where there was cocaine. I had gone up to do a security buy. That's when you're a kind of advance man for the tactical team that's going to kick down the door and arrest everybody. The security man goes in first to make a drug buy, check out who's there and what kinds of arms and drugs they're holding. I approached the place. They were selling through a screened

" I don't need to be patted on the back, because I know I'm doing a good job.
Out there on the street, you know, the propensity for violence is extremely high, but its probability is
extremely low. So you keep that in your mind to push down the apprehension and the stress that's doing
its best to rise up."

Peter Hendrie

*"The undercover officers have a lot more fear dealing with the young fifteen-
and sixteen-year-old pushers than they do with the adults, because the young ones are very immature and
fearless. They're much more carefree about using a gun. It's like a new toy to them, and they're eager
to try it out."*

window. Basically, what you'd do is hand in the money through a small opening. The seller is behind a curtain so you can't identify him when he passes the dope. When I walked up, he ID'd me as a cop and wouldn't sell to me. But he had already sold to some people who were right in front of me. He pulled the curtain back so I got a clear view of his face, and then we got into a big screaming match using a bunch of four-letter words. Everybody on the streets nearby could hear us. I didn't know it, but at the time, he had a .357 magnum pointed directly at me. When the tactical team kicked the door down, they found it fully loaded. Situations like this seem pretty serious at the time, but when you look back at them, you just kinda crack up. Me and my partner used to get into lots of humorous jams like this. There we are, two white boys in a totally black community, and we're shucking and jiving with these guys — situations like that.

Probably in the past two months alone we've taken down some seventy houses. Just about every other house we've been in has had one or two weapons in it. These guys are trying to protect their dope and their money, because they get robbed just like anyone else. So when we walk into a dope house, they'll often point a gun at us and say, "Are you police?" They think that if we answer no, we can't bust them.

I usually carry two guns in these situations, concealing them the best I can. One's a five-shot .38-caliber revolver, and the other's a nine-millimeter sixteen-shot automatic pistol. Occasionally they try to frisk me, but you use your wits and tell them to back off. "You don't touch me, and I won't touch you." You just kinda move away from them, and they seem to understand. You just use whatever bullshit line and all the wits you've got to keep things going.

I've never had to use my gun in a situation yet. If I ever had to, I would. But the fact is we see a lot more bravado than gunplay in these situations. As they say, "Miami vice is nothing like 'Miami Vice,' " or any of the other police shows that are on television for that matter.

My schedule is a bigger killer than the gunplay I see out there. My wife's a police officer as well. We both work extremely long hours. We're away from home a lot. My wife works days, so we're like ships passing in the night. And that can cause the occasional shipwreck. When she's going to work, I'm asleep, and when she gets home, I'm off to work, so we don't have a heck of a lot of conversations. That's a problem, and so is the fact I don't get to see my kids all that much.

Even given problems at home and the stress and the burnout, I'll probably remain in narcotics a while longer. At least until the dealers start recognizing me. You figure you can change your looks as often as possible, but sooner or later, particularly if you're out there making two and three deals a day, they'll get your number.

It's not fear that I carry around, but a kind of unrelenting stress and apprehension. Going out and buying drugs and making deals only takes about fifteen minutes. The biggest part of my job is paperwork, filing cases and cranking out reports. Most of the time I'm more under the gun to get that stuff done and presented to the prosecutor than I am from any dealer. There's an enormous amount of paperwork, and it creates stress that just climbs on top of the apprehension you're already feeling from undercover work. It's not a matter of being afraid or scared or anything. It's just the constant stress that's on you day in and day out.

You can't help taking your work home with you. You can't get it out of your head, the rough times, when people have held guns to you. You're totally alone and if they want, they can kill you at any time. They can do it! You're there all by yourself, and you're acting macho, using all your wits to talk these people down. It's just braver bullshit that you're applying in these situations.

If I'm not out buying dope, the guys on the uniform side are sitting on their hands, because they won't have any search warrants to execute. So the pressure's always on. At any moment I'll have about eight case files open, and I'll be processing papers to get warrants issued against people I've bought drugs from. Once the warrants are issued, the uniformed cops can move and usually arrest five or six people at each house for possession of narcotics, conspiracy to sell, or whatever. I really feel the need to process those papers fast!

My experience with juvenile dealers is that they're more greedy because they get a cut, and they're eager to sell to anybody and everybody. So they're easier to buy from. They're also a little bit crazy and have no fear of the gun, so to speak. Some of them are as violent or more violent than many adults. We tend not to focus on the juvenile dealers as much, only because we're mostly after the big guys who are supplying them. Also, these kids get sent through the juvenile courts, and in most instances they are back out on the streets within hours of their arrests.

My job's a good one. I thoroughly enjoy putting dealers in jail. I don't need to be patted on the back, because I know I'm doing a good job. Out there on the street, you know, the propensity for violence is extremely high, but its probability is extremely low. So you keep that in your mind to push down the apprehension and the stress that's doing its best to rise up. I could give a thousand reasons why this job is bad, but I'm helping society and that outweighs all of them. It's important to me! It's the way I've been all my life.

■

Crack is our main problem right now. It's widespread. It's in every part of town. The highest concentrations of crack cocaine are at retail outlets located in the inner city, especially in lower-income neighborhoods around the public housing areas. Most of the sales are overt and open. A lot of street dealers are operating out there, and they are ruining whole communities. The homicide rate is jumping, and the whole situation is just pretty overwhelming right now. Kansas City is probably not in as bad shape as some cities closer to the coasts where drugs are shipped in more easily, but the stuff is all about.

For us a big seizure is a pound of

"You can't help taking your work home with you. You can't get it out of your head, the rough times. You're totally alone and if they want, they can kill you at any time… you're acting macho, using all your wits to talk these people down. It's just braver bullshit that you're applying."

cocaine. That's sizable. Whereas in Miami or California, that's considered a minor bust. Our problems are not the big shipments, but the petty transactions, the retail sales, and all the extracurricular activity that goes along with it — the feuds between dope dealers and the fighting within the neighborhoods. And it's the older people on fixed incomes who suffer most in this hostile environment. The neighborhood goes down the drain to the dope dealers who've moved in.

One time, I snuck up on some guys doing street deals. It turned out to be two twelve-year-old kids, both of whom had sizable amounts of cocaine on them. One kid told us he worked for the other twelve-year-old selling dope but that he was almost at the point where he could start employing his own force of peewee pushers. It's a pretty sad state of affairs.

The state of the court system doesn't make it much better. The courts are overworked and so glutted with a tremendous influx of cases that only the biggest and best cases are picked, which sends the wrong message to the public. Dope dealers get arrested, but a short time later they're back out and never seem to get charged down the road. With this going on, it gets difficult to make people believe that crime doesn't pay anymore. The drug dealers start to think, "Gosh, even if you get caught by the police, nothing happens." This is one of the reasons the number of drug pushers just keeps on rising, especially the younger ones who are prosecuted through an extremely lenient juvenile court. Lots of times dealers intentionally employ kids under the age of seventeen to sell dope. Even if they're caught, nothing happens to them. When you're nabbing them, these kids will even scream out, "You can't do anything to me, I'm a juvenile!" So true, so true.

The undercover officers have a lot more fear dealing with the young fifteen- and sixteen-year-old pushers than they do with the adults, because the young ones are very immature and fearless. They're much more carefree about using a gun. It's like a new toy to them, and they're eager to try it out.

Unlike the midlevel and upper-level drug traffickers, who are very organized, with set rules on how to do business, the street-level guys are very disorganized. It's all very informal, and the players are fast changing. We'll go into a dope house and buy from a dealer. But often, by the time we return with a search warrant, there's a whole new cast of characters there. So maybe in one out of five cases, we won't nail the guy we identified earlier.

I've been a policeman in Kansas City for ten years and with another department for five. From my experience, the community here gives us the highest level of support. It's especially true in the inner city. The support is rock solid there. The impact of crack cocaine in these communities is devastating. The people in the inner city are living the catastrophe first hand.

But even upper-middle-class kids in the suburbs find it acceptable. It's a vestige of the early 1980s when coke was kinda the cool thing to do. So some of these goofies are still playing with it. They never really grew up. Then you've got the young kids pushing this garbage down in the inner city. Because everyone's doing it. It's not criminal in their eyes. They look at it as the hip thing to do. Make some fast money. Wear some flashy jewelry. Even buy yourself a new car. We've got kids here too young for driver's licenses, but they own sleek cars.

One twerp just turned seventeen, and he had all these grown-ups and older kids dealing his dope. He was a mini-mob figure, driving around in the back of a taxi cab with his little entourage. He'd wear gold chains around his neck and gold rings on every finger. He made Mr. T look like he'd taken vows of poverty. I mean, this kid wore gold! He must've had backaches just from wearing that junk all day.

We were anxious to nail him because he was a walking advertisement, recruiting other kids and ruining the neighborhood. But we couldn't get a case on him. He was smart and never had dope on him, always had someone else carry it. As an uneducated teenager, he was pretty impressive in his line of work,

but he was kind of a hateful little creature. The area in which he operated was a little war zone. There were drive-by shootings and all kinds of feuds. Finally he got into a run-in with some folks, and he fire-bombed their house, killing five or six people, including kids and old people. At last we nailed him on something, and he's now in the county jail awaiting trial. A serious menace is off the streets, for the time being at least!

Dealing with the crooks day in, day out can get depressing, particularly if you can't get them on anything. So you have to be creative! Sometimes we see a street dealer throw away his bag of dope as we approach. We can't arrest him for drug possession unless a field test has been done, so we'll get him on littering, until a lab test returns and confirms it's crack cocaine. We'll nickel-dime him to death — get him for not having a registration sticker on his windshield or no front license plate on his car. We'll get his car towed, and if he's dealing in a public housing project where he doesn't live, we'll get the management to sign a complaint for trespassing. We'll just keep on building up the minor charges against him, and eventually the city judges will get sick of seeing his face, see the trend, and put him on the municipal farm for six months, give him a taste of the real time he's going to get if he keeps it up.

Occasionally judges will do this kind of thing, but in general the legal system has its problems. Its main function seems to be to employ lawyers and not serve up justice. Victims and witnesses go into court, and most times they get victimized by defense attorneys who can huff and puff and say anything they want about them. Most of these people are timid about being witnesses in the first place. They're not used to the hostility, and they get startled when they discover that they're treated like suspects when cross-examined. They find it demeaning. I've got a lot of respect for the witnesses who have the courage to follow through with it. The courts leave something to be desired. They're not cordial at all to the decent people.

We have problems for sure in some of our housing projects. Two patrol cars will go to an incident, and they might return with their tires slashed and their windows busted. It happens on occasion. People have taken potshots at the windows, done stuff like that. It may not sound as bad as it is in other cities, but it's the worst I have seen in fifteen years of law enforcement.

In the past I've thought, "Gosh, it can't get much worse than this." That was when I was in narcotics and PCP was on the rampage. Then there were these laced marijuana cigarettes that created instant psychos. That was wild, and I thought, "This has got to be the worst!" But then along comes crack, and "worst" is redefined! It's not only truly bad, but it's everywhere.

Go down to our projects, especially in the evening hours, and you'll see license plates of cars coming from middle-class and upper-middle-class suburban communities. They spin by the projects to buy their dope. These people don't belong there. They don't know where they're going. They don't know what they're doing. And they make such easy victims. They're not doing business with some Joe in a pinstripe suit at the bank. They're doing transactions with the lowest form of commerce, junkies souped up on crack, who don't have an ounce of respect for themselves or those they're dealing with. It's no big thing for this kinda guy to pop off a buyer, even if he's from the suburbs.

One of the things that kinda irritates me is that the media keep calling people who use cocaine and other drugs "substance abuse victims." I don't care if they're from the projects or some lush suburb, they're junkies. They're not victims of the problem. They're part of the problem. And the sooner we quit making excuses for them, the better. They're immature and irresponsible people. And when they get caught, they'll inevitably fall back on "Oh, my, but I'm a victim! Cut me some slack."

I just don't think we should be cutting any slack on this deal. They're crooks, and every time they buy dope, they're committing a felony. If these suburban junkies weren't cruising down here to cop smack, these kids in the projects wouldn't be selling it. No clientele, no business!

It seems like everyone's getting lackadaisical and overly sympathetic about this. Society better wake up, 'cause the homicide rate is rising, and it includes little kids and old ladies and poor guys who happen to be at the wrong place at the wrong time when goofies cut loose with automatic and semiautomatic weapons. These are shooters — little gangsters, really — who don't exactly go to the range every day for target practice. They're not real proficient marksmen. They just kinda spray the whole area and hope it hits the right guy. Unfortunately, that right guy might be the wrong guy — it just might be you or your wife or your kids.

It's a hard, hard world we're moving into! Eventually everyone is going to be wearing body armor and living in fortresses if nothing's done. And we're raising a generation of monsters, and each generation is getting more and more violent. Out on the street, we've got fourteen- and fifteen-year-old kids who are fathering children. Totally immature kids are passing on totally immature values and morals.

"My schedule is a bigger killer than the gunplay I see out there. My wife's a police officer as well. We both work extremely long hours. We're away from home a lot. My wife works days, so we're like ships passing in the night. And that can cause the occasional shipwreck."

Radar Enforcement

Shreveport, Louisiana

"People will do anything to beat that ticket. They'll test our patience and call us names, do anything they can. Part of our job is to stomach the abuse. We take it as a kind of challenge to match them word-for-word with smiles."

Peter Hendrie

"You might be sitting out there running a little radar and the person you stop
for speeding turns out to have just robbed the bank down the road. You just don't know what that car
coming down the highway is going to bring you."

We have a little trick around here for computing who's running red lights. You need to know a little mathematics, but all the officers get it sooner or later. We position our motorcycles in a spot where we can monitor the traffic on a given street. We know the cycle of the stoplights, so even if we can't directly see the light seen by the approaching motorists we're monitoring, we know when their light turns red. That's because the opposite light, which is turning green, is in our direct view. We start the stopwatch the moment their light turns red and stop it when the vehicle gets to the edge of the intersection. This gives us an elapsed time to work with: the half second or so it takes the car to reach the intersection, once the light turned red, plus the normal three-second yellow phase of the light prior to its turning red. The officer with this timing can now compute the number of feet away from the intersection the vehicle was when the light turned red and prove that it did, indeed, run it.

He can do this because he knows that the maximum speed the car should be traveling in the area is 40 mph — that's the same as sixty feet per second. He multiplies his elapsed time by sixty feet per second to show just where the car was during phases of the stoplight. This is important in court as backup evidence to his visual sighting of the violation. The red-light runner will likely be screaming that the light was still yellow, but simple mathematics proves him wrong.

Radar is one of the principal devices we use, and it's definitely here to stay. It's been challenged in the courts, but it's now accepted for what it is. A properly trained officer can use it effectively, and it's far more advanced than it was in the beginning. The fallacy of the moving trees, houses, and such was never there. It was simple operator error, but we now train our officers to work them well. It's my understanding that a new system of laser radar is being developed that will be even more difficult to detect.

Radar detectors aren't a big problem, just another challenge. They're a game for our

Peter Hendrie

officers, more than a test for the radar. Our motorcycle cops often visually estimate the speed of cars prior to actually turning on the radar gun. By doing this, they fool the people with radar detectors. It's too late by the time the people pick up radar. Our cops get a kick out of beating these guys and their fancy technology.

I've dropped my motorcycle more times than I can remember. I've torn up six or eight good motorcycles. Even crashed one going 87 mph. That bike was well-designed and saved me quite a bit. The crash bars kept me from being hurt real bad. I've gotten broadsided and knocked-out for two days. I've hit an oil slick and a curb. I've lost skin all over, even broken my neck. All your motorcycle incidents, all the close calls, they've all happened to me at least once. I have a lot of cuts and bruises and mangled motorcycles to show these new cops I train. These guys are benefiting a lot from the experience of my mishaps. I don't have an overwhelming urge to ride a desk, but I do it about half the time now. The other half I'm out on the street. My role has changed from doing what I'm told to do to telling others what they're supposed to do.

When you're out on the street, you get all kinds of excuses. Some will say, "I was speeding because I had to get to a bathroom," or "I was just trying to keep up with all the other cars that were hurrying." Others will whine, "What about all those other speeding cars? Don't just pick on me!" People are always trying to justify their actions, grasping for a credible excuse rather than admitting they were wrong. They're like small children. Whatever the case, be it speeding or running a red light, they just keep cooking up the same routine excuses.

We get some people multiple times. They just never learn. I've nailed individuals twice in one day for the same violation. You try to give them as much benefit as you can, but sometimes they really don't give you any option. They bring it on themselves.

We get all attitudes! We'll get individuals that are belligerent and uncooperative.

They just don't want you to do your job. Then we'll get the complacent ones. They won't say a word, they'll just sit there and co-operate, admit everything. You have to treat all of them the same, as individuals, and not let attitudes determine if you write them a ticket or not.

People will do anything to beat that ticket. They'll test our patience and call us names, do anything they can. We try our best to maintain composure and act professional. If we do, nine times out of ten we come out with the upper hand. But if we lose composure and succumb to the temptation to name call as well or act unprofessionally, then the problems grow. Part of our job is to stomach the abuse. We take it as a kind of challenge to match them word-for-word with smiles. At the same time we're writing down pretty much everything that's said so it can be used against the violator if the case goes to court.

Occasionally, we'll get the other extreme from abuse — the woman who offers sexual favors to beat the ticket. It does come up from time to time. The majority of cops work here from seven in the morning to seven in the evening, so they don't have the opportunity to take these people up on such offers. I've been approached numerous times, but who's got time?

It's not actually the radar that usually convicts them in court, it's the visual estimate made by the police officer. We go to school to learn how to visually gauge within two miles per hour the speed of cars before we're certified to operate radar here in Louisiana. It's hard to do. When you go to court, you'll be asked, "What brought this vehicle to your attention, officer?" You say, "Well, I made a visual estimate of 68 mph." Then the district attorney might say, "Did you confirm your visual estimate?" "Yes, Sir, I used a K15 hand gun." "And what did the radar show?" "Seventy mph." So it wasn't the radar that convicted that person. It was the visual estimate.

I was in a 25-mph residential area yesterday. I had my helmet off and was standing beside my motorcycle. These two guys in a Chevrolet passed another car, which is against the law in a residential area. They were doing forty when I jumped out and screamed, "Hey, hey, come back here." They just looked at me and took off with a full bore of smoke coming out of their tail pipe. I ran for my motorcycle, trying to get my helmet on and my ticket book and radar gun stashed. By the time I was rolling, they'd run a red light, turned down a side street, and crossed a woman's yard. They were gone. A while later, another motorcycle officer chased them, but they got away again. You've got to be careful in the rush to get them. You don't know what they've done, and you don't want to get hurt. They might have robbed a bank, or they might have a little dope. Turns out the car was stolen; that's why they were running so fast.

I've lost a bit of bark out there in motorcycle accidents. Oh, I've probably left several inches of skin on the road in my time. I've had three wrecks and two knee operations. The first dump was in October of '87. I was after someone and was doing about 80 mph trying to pull him over. There was a piece of concrete about eighteen inches in diameter just lying on the road. I hit it, went straight in the air and came down hard. I laid the bike over and skidded with it about three hundred yards. I lost a lot of the skin on my arm, and these keys that I wear, one of them got jammed up on my hip. It sort of knocked me silly. The guy I was chasing stopped, too, just to check me out.

Needless to say, when the emergency people came, they stripped me down. We've got a saying in the department, "Always wear clean underwear to work, 'cause, you never know." That's the first thing they do, you know, they take off your clothes.

The second one happened in May of '88. I was pulling a guy over, and I hit a crack with the front tire. The bike flipped. One minute I was up. The next, I was down. It broke my left leg below the knee. I got slapped in the hospital for eight days and had extensive knee surgery. I recuperated after

several months.

The third accident happened a few months later that same year. I was riding along on my motorcycle, minding my own business, when a gentleman pulled out in front of me. I didn't see him at all. The collision severed my lip real bad; it actually cut my lip off. I hit the hood. I hit the windshield. I bounced on the street. It tore the motorcycle up real bad. I reinjured my leg and had to have more surgery.

My wife tends to worry about me and motorcycles. When I leave early in the morning, tears well up in her eyes. She doesn't say anything direct to me like, "I wish you'd get out of it," but she worries all the time. Three times now she's answered the phone to hear, "Ma'am, your husband's been involved in a motorcycle accident and he's in the hospital. Can you come right down?" They never tell you how smashed up he is, just, "Come on over, now." She's always expecting that phone to ring again.

Most of this job has nothing to do with risks and danger. Once I was watching the traffic and a white doodlebug Volkswagen came flying through, going about seventy. The Volkswagen was so full of junk, you couldn't even see a driver. It was crammed with furniture, clothes, old suitcases, you name it. When I finally got the subject pulled over, I walked up to the car and, believe it or not, this twenty-one- or twenty-two-year-old college girl is sitting there stark nude. She's wearing nothing more than her birthday suit, and it's a well-cut job at that! I asked the young lady why she didn't have any clothes on, and she said she had no air conditioning and it was hot. So it all flustered me a bit, and I was turning red. I didn't know what to do, so I started writing a ticket. Finally, I muddled through and told her to stop at the next gas station and put some clothes on. Then I let her go. The really funny thing is when I looked at my ticket book later, I discovered I'd forgotten to write her name or her license plate number down. I had Volkswagen and the street where we had stopped, even how fast she was going. But the ticket was worthless; I had no way to

trace her.

Sometimes we'll get women who will try to bribe you with their pleasures. If a male officer stops them, they'll show their breasts. I had one once who I'd stopped for speeding. She got out of the car, and all she was wearing was an extremely loose men's shirt. The passing truckers got a kick out of it. They steered over into the right lane and blew her shirt up so that they got to see all that nothing underneath. I wrote her a ticket anyway. She ought to have known better.

People don't like to get tickets. That shouldn't come as a big surprise. I've asked folks to sign when they're receiving one, and they'll throw my ticket book into the street. I've had them throw my pens as well. I've been called a lot of names. I've had a lot of black people say the reason you're stopping me is because I'm black. But then on the other hand, I've had a lot of white people say to me the only reason you're stopping me is because I'm driving a red sports car and you don't like red sports cars. Some people have even complained to internal affairs about me after I've given them tickets. I've been investigated. But I've been cleared every time. People just don't like getting tickets. And tickets tend to bring out the absolute worst in them.

I've never had a real fight with the folks I pull over for normal traffic violations. A couple of them have come at me in a threatening manner, but it hasn't lasted. I've gotten into fights with drunk drivers, and I got into one in which another officer had to come help. A drunk had been playing basketball. He was a big tall guy, and he was strung out. We fought so hard on a two-story porch, it fell off the house, and we fell about twenty feet to the ground. I finally wrestled him into jail.

One of our officers lost his life just recently. He'd pulled a van over on the road, sensing it might be transporting illegal contraband. The narcotics detail was rushed to the scene, and a number of officers were busy checking out the car.

In a bad coincidence, this guy who was a mental case happened to be passing by in his car. The man had been involved in an incident two weeks earlier in which he rammed several police cars. He had been booked on drunk driving and destruction of property and then released. But it seems he'd really been trying to kill himself. So when he saw the officers standing on the road dealing with the stopped vehicle, he just careened into two patrol cars and hit an officer head-on, sheering his legs off. He died a little later. The guy who hit him ended up a suicide a few weeks later in a jail cell. Some kind of justice may have been served on this one.

I was a pallbearer at the officer's funeral and it hurt. It's a painful honor particularly when you're close. We all stick together pretty much. I've been to three funerals for police officers over the years. If you ever have to go to one, you'll find it the saddest experience there is.

Statistically, there are probably more traffic cops killed than patrol officers, for the simple reason that traffic cops don't know who they're stopping. You might be sitting out there running a little radar and the person you stop for speeding turns out to have just robbed the bank down the road. You may not know it, and end up in serious risk. You just don't know what that car coming down the highway is going to bring you.

Assault

Tulsa, Oklahoma

"If it's a simple assault, you'll talk with them gently, get them quieted down, and get the information you need for the report. Occasionally, you just hold their hand and talk about whatever concerns them at that frightening moment."

When we get the call from the dispatcher, we pepper him with questions. Where's the suspect? What shape's he in? How's the victim? Is anyone armed? We're totally dependent on the dispatcher in assessing the assault.

Assault in this business can be anything from one person punching another out to fatal stabbings and shootings. If it's a simple assault, I collect the facts and write up a report. Doesn't take much time at all. If it's major assault, I'll be hung up awhile. For those, we usually call detectives and a scientific investigations unit to the scene to take photos and collect evidence.

Most typically, your assaults are triggered by domestic disputes. The husband or live-in boyfriend has assaulted the female. He might have hit the victim in the face with his fist or with some makeshift weapon, a vase, a beer bottle, or anything else that's handy. In a recent case, I had a woman turn the tables and haul off and slug her boyfriend.

Another time, a ten-year-old newspaper boy on his bike shouted something that irked a passing group of high school students. The older boys came back and knocked him off his bicycle and beat him severely. Both his eyes were blackened and swollen shut, and he needed stitches to close a gash in his forehead. It's disturbing. You've got to wonder why a group of teenagers would assault a little boy.

If I'm called to a highly charged scene, a brawl in a bar, for example, I'll ask the dispatcher how far away the backup units are. I might even wait for other officers to arrive before going in. You're less likely to be injured if you enter in numbers.

We're not supermen, you know. We're not going to just charge in there playing John Wayne and say, "Okay, break it up! Everybody up against the wall!" How much good can I do if I run in there, get jumped and clobbered in the head with a chair? Other officers would just have to come in and rescue me.

Assault knows no income level or color. It runs the gamut. Working in a very wealthy part of town, I responded to a complaint about

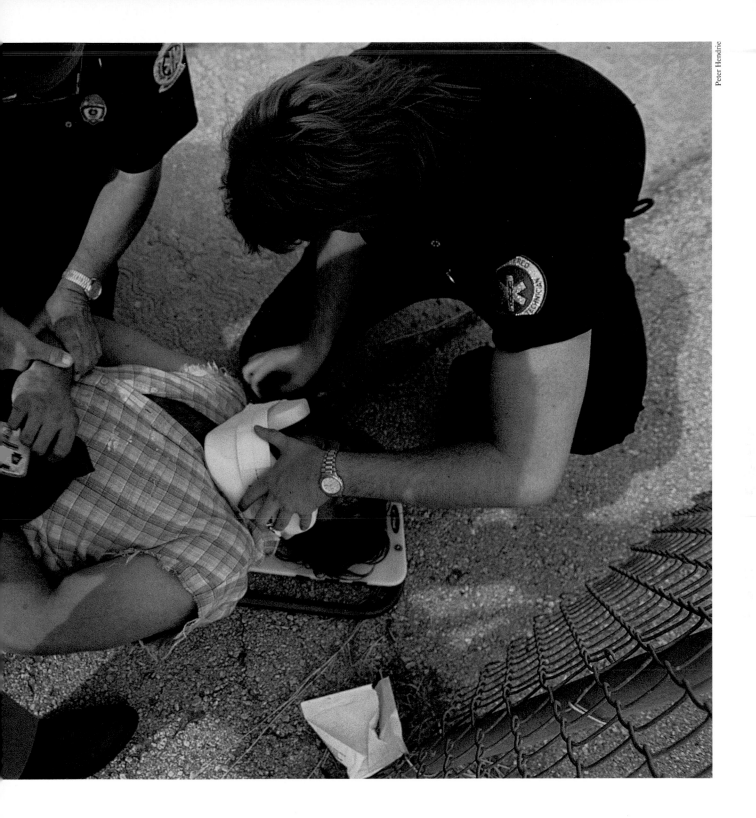

"Assaults occur on every socioeconomic level. The difference is that in the rich part of town we don't get called on. It's an embarrassment to them. In the lower-income areas, people don't have the money to resolve their problems themselves or with specialized help. Thus they turn to us."

a man and woman who had just assaulted each other. They turned out to be well-to-do, and each was waving a gun at the other. As nice as they seemed, they had guns, and the potential was there to be killed or seriously wounded in the heat of the moment.

The response we get at the scene of a crime can vary widely. Some are glad to see us, and they're counting on us to resolve a complex, heated dispute. But others will inevitably be hissing under their breaths, or sometimes even shouting, "You're just going to bring us more grief." This is particularly true if we're about to haul one of the parties off to the slammer.

Usually the scene of an assault is somewhat chaotic, and people are charged up. They're all screaming, "This guy did it! That guy did it! He should go to jail! Lock him up! Why don't you cuff him?" Most of the time, in fact, it takes quite a bit of questioning to sort out the players and determine who actually did what to whom. I tend to duck the insults that often get thrown at me. My police uniform is my skin. It's just a little thicker than the normal person's. Verbal abuse comes with the job. We learn that lesson in training. If we didn't, we couldn't survive on the streets.

■

Surprisingly, in Tulsa, female officers don't seem to work so many rape cases. Maybe that's because rape cases are assigned randomly here, regardless of the sex of the investigator. If the victim requires a woman, then we'll go out. I've been in the department four years, and I've probably responded to as many rapes in that time. The last such case was a young lady in one of the housing complexes. Nobody came to her aid as she ran, naked and in terror, from door to door calling for help. By the time we got there, she had beat on so many doors her hands were bruised. It kind of worries me that something like this could happen in Tulsa.

Often, it's kids who get assaulted by grown-ups. We had one case in South Tulsa where the father disciplined his son a bit too hard. He was whipping the kid's legs and back with a switch off a tree. The child was taken from the father and placed in a home.

At the scene of an assault, you always try to be particularly sensitive to the victim. Sometimes, if it's a simple assault, you'll talk with them gently, get them quieted down, and get the information you need for the report. Occasionally, you just hold their hand and talk about whatever concerns them at that frightening moment.

■

When I send an officer out to a crime, whatever the circumstances, I insist he treat people the way he would want to be treated himself in that situation.

I also always insist that my officers take a backup on assaults. If we can't take control of a situation without getting hurt ourselves, we're not doing our job right. The more officers you can put at a scene — regardless of whether it's a husband and wife going at it or a bar brawl — the less likely there's going to be physical violence.

The biggest change around here is that we no longer look at assaults as being routine and unavoidable. For example, three or four years ago we had a strip of eight bars in one block. A wave of assaults and strong-arm robberies was occurring in the vicinity of these bars. We met with people in the community, and they started complaining to the bar owners about letting their patrons get too drunk. Before long, the bars were declared a public nuisance and a court order was issued that they be moved and not be allowed to congregate in one location. It solved the assault problem completely.

But don't be fooled. Assaults occur on every socioeconomic level. The difference is that in the rich part of town we don't get called on. It's an embarrassment to them. In the lower-income areas, people don't have the money to resolve their problem themselves or with specialized help. Thus they turn to us.

"I tend to duck the insults that often get thrown at me. My police uniform is my skin. It's just a little thicker than the normal person's. Verbal abuse comes with the job. We learn that lesson in training. If we didn't, we couldn't survive on the streets."

Residential Burglary

Dallas, Texas

"We tell our officers that the most important thing to remember at a burglary scene is to be compassionate… Burglaries are an emotional experience for the victim… All of us are possessive and proud of our things, and if in fifteen minutes some SOB takes all those things you cherish, it's a crushing experience."

Over the past decade new buildings have popped up everywhere, and the city has grown by leaps and bounds. But guess what? Burglary has kept right up with it. It's got to be one of the worst problems that Dallas is confronting.

The burglary rate in many areas of the city has gone sky high. Drugs are on the upsurge, and they're the reason for most of our burglaries. And it's not just crack, but all the other drugs they're taking — like heroin and cocaine. People don't keep the stuff they steal anymore, like they did in the old days. They sell it to make money to feed their habits.

This may sound trivial, but we tell our officers that the most important thing to remember at a burglary scene is to be compassionate. After a few years of experience, police officers have a tendency to become somewhat mechanical and unemotional about their work. It's mostly a defense mechanism. But burglaries are an emotional experience for the victim. A lot of times the first thing they yell is, "Where the hell were you guys?" and "What took you so long?" Sometimes it's a bit hard to handle. But all of us are possessive and proud of our things, and if in fifteen minutes some SOB takes all those things you cherish, it's a crushing experience. People have equated burglary with rape, because of the feeling of absolute violation. The victim's emotional and wants to talk with a police officer who is compassionate and caring. Cops sometimes forget this, because most haven't been victims themselves. At the scene, they might be too methodical: "Okay, where were you?" "How long were you gone?" "When did it happen?" "Have you got any information on the suspect?" "Give me a list of what was stolen." "What was the total dollar amount stolen?" "Thank you, good-bye." That's when people really get angry.

Most burglaries are boring. They're very routine, and police officers end up being little more than report takers. The unusual ones are the suspicious ones. You find no signs of forced entry, nothing is broken, nothing is

" One time I spent the whole night looking for a burglar who'd broken into this lady's house… Seventy-seven years old, on social security, and he still took her TV… If you're only getting three hundred dollars in social security per month, it's real hard. It's an unbelievable feeling when you walk back into that woman's house and say, 'Here, I've recovered your property.' "

"When you catch a burglar inside a building, nine times out of ten he's not going to try to escape. But catch him outside, and it's chase time. You have to run and run and run… Sometimes, it's a toss-up of who's going to win."

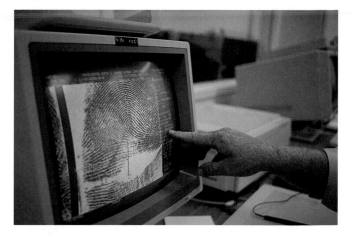

out of place. The victim swears the house was locked. And then, all of a sudden, a ten-thousand-dollar diamond necklace is missing. The first thing that crosses your mind is insurance fraud. When you're walking out the door, the victim just keeps repeating, "Now remember, I need a copy of this for my insurance company."

If burglaries are going to be reduced, people have to be more aware of how to safeguard their property. Some of them walk out the door and forget to lock it, often intentionally. "Oh, I always leave the back door open because my daughter's coming home from school." Or they think they're only going down to the local store for fifteen minutes to get a pack of cigarettes, only to come back hours later to find their house burglarized. People get lulled into a false sense of security. It's like car wrecks — it only happens to the other guy.

If they can afford them, alarm systems serve as deterrents to burglary. Often an alarm system won't stop the burglary, but it'll make such a racket that the burglar moves on to an easier target. Remember, they don't want to come into contact with people. They want to get in and get out without confrontation.

Catching a burglar in the act is a great experience. About the only thing that tops it is nabbing an armed robber. Most of the time, when the officers arrive at a burglary, the suspect has long since gone. But if you're lucky and get the call when you're right around the corner, you can get there in time. Thankfully, the burglars that I've come in direct contact with haven't been armed, though more and

more of them are today. It's so easy to get a gun in this city. There's even been a proliferation of weapons in private hands. People are afraid and want to protect themselves. These are folks who just ten years ago were saying, "I'd never own a gun." Now they're buying them.

Perhaps the wackiest burglary that's occurred was one where the guy went through the window, cooked a steak dinner, and sat down and watched TV. Naturally, he took the TV with him when he left. That was a funny one! We had another where the guy just ate a gallon of ice cream and then split. He left the ice cream container lying on the bed. Guess he was pretty hungry. Later we found out it was a man who was trying to scare the woman who owned the place, to get back at her.

When it looks like an inside job, I'll usually pass it on to the investigators. Like today, this guy had a key. It was obvious he had a key to the house that was burglarized. Things weren't taken that the normal burglar would have taken. I knew it immediately! When I said to the woman whose residence had been burglarized, "How did they get in?" She said, "I don't know. Everything was locked up." It so happened that the only person who knew that the doors were locked was her husband. I asked her, "When you got home, was he here?" "No, he called me." It all added up. She knew who it was! She knew exactly who it was when I asked, "Do you know what I'm thinking?" I asked her about her divorce and whether it was bitter. In a lot of divorces, a party thinks: "This object is mine. It belongs to me, so I'm going to take it, even if I have to break in to get it." I've seen that happen quite a bit. It might not be retaliatory, just something that he felt he owned even though the judge had awarded it to her. "That's okay. I'll just walk in and take it. I've got the key!"

When you catch your typical burglar, he's usually very cooperative, because he knows the spot he's in. Residential burglary is a first-degree felony here. A serious crime! So most times, he comes quietly.

When you catch a burglar inside a building, nine times out of ten he's not going to try to escape. But catch him outside, and it's chase time. You have to run and run and run. When you catch up with him, you're tired and he's tired. I try to keep in good physical condition for just this kind of thing. Sometimes, it's a toss-up of who's going to win at that point. If you win, he goes to jail. If he wins, he gets away. Knock on wood, so far I haven't lost one yet.

We had a burglar jump off the top of a building, take an officer's gun, and shoot. You can never anticipate such violence. You never know if they are armed or not. You can take a thousand precautions, and it's never enough. Often, you get in a physical confrontation, and you just don't have room to escape.

I tend to think that burglary is as bad as violent crime. I've seen how it affects people. You go to some retired person's house, and there they are, sitting and crying because they've lost the only television they had, and they sit there and cry for days because now they've got nothing else to do but sit and look at the bare walls. You become prejudiced toward burglars. They become the lowest thing on earth at that moment. But you get over it.

One time I spent the whole night looking for a burglar who'd broken into this lady's house. By the end of my shift I found the guy, and I arrested him. That lady was seventy-seven years old, on social security, and he still took her TV. No way was I going to let him get away with that.

Officers are particularly sensitive toward elderly people and the young, who are just starting out. If you have a job that pays a hundred thousand dollars a year, well, you can replace that TV. But if you're only getting three hundred dollars in social security per month, it's real hard. In those situations, you try your very best to find the thief. It's an unbelievable feeling when you walk back into that woman's house and say, "Here, I've recovered your property." Then you go home and tell your family, "Hey, look what I did today." The job has its moments, it does!

Vehicle Stops

Lakewood, Colorado

"A high-risk stop might be required at any moment… We might just be out in the patrol car and see someone displaying a gun or even holding it to somebody's head. We often get 'rolling domestics.' This is when a man and woman are fighting behind the wheel, and he is waving a weapon at her while cruising."

"We're stopping so many people for reasons that aren't felonies but which are definitely high-risk… situations where people's emotions are running high, they're out of control, and they may be carrying a weapon.   If a policeman is confronting a drunk with a gun, and particularly if he's in a two-or three-thousand-pound vehicle — that's high-risk."

ormal vehicle stops can be potentially threatening to us, but high-risk ones are considered outright dangerous. Usually, when we pull a car over in such a situation, the occupant is suspected of a crime or of carrying firearms. Our primary consideration in the maneuver is the safety of the officers involved. Normally we do not make high-risk vehicle stops with less than two patrol cars, and preferably with three or four. We always choose carefully where we make the stop. Obviously, we prefer well-lit areas, but those away from pedestrians and other vehicle traffic. We'll normally have at the ready the shotguns we carry in most of the patrol cars. I've made dozens of such high-risk stops, and I still get anxious. You just don't know what might happen.

We think we're adept at stopping vehicles, but sometimes things just don't work out the way you've planned. We had an incident a few months ago in which one of our officers pulled over a vehicle for a burnt-out taillight. It wasn't a high-risk stop, but the driver bolted out of the truck and fled on foot. The officer chased him all the way around a residential area, but somehow the guy managed to duck back to where they'd started.

The dejected officer was in the process of returning to her car. As she walked up the street, she looked up and said to herself, "That's funny, the street is awfully dark, but I left my overhead emergency lights on. They should be illuminating the street, but where are they?" She yelled out to some bystanders, "Did you see that man I was chasing?"

"Sure did," said one. "He just left in your patrol car." Well, it was pretty embarrassing for the officer. She'd only been a cop for a month.

When the police finally picked up the guy, he was dead drunk and about a block away from the abandoned patrol car. He kept repeating that he had been trying to report his own car stolen but there was no record of any such call to the police station. His story was just full of holes.

We booked him for two DUIs — one for driving his own car under the influence and a second count for driving a patrol car. A happy ending to a story that could have had pretty severe consequences if the drunk had carried a weapon.

■

We used to call them felony vehicle stops, but the department is trying to get away from that. High-risk vehicle stops is how we describe them now. It's because we're stopping so many people for reasons that aren't felonies but which are definitely high-risk. For example, situations where people's emotions are running high, they're out of control, and they may be carrying a weapon. In Colorado, or anywhere else for that matter, if a policeman is confronting a drunk with a gun, and particularly if he's in a two- or three-thousand-pound vehicle — that's high-risk.

We're telling the officer to be more vigilant; do everything to avoid potential injury and don't take chances. The little old lady whose car you're approaching might just be off the handle and waving a fully loaded automatic.

A high-risk stop might be required at any moment. A citizen will call in that someone's driving around brandishing a pistol. A bad guy might be seen leaving the scene of a crime. We might just be out in the patrol car and see someone displaying a gun or even holding it to somebody's head. We often get "rolling domestics." This is when a man and woman are fighting behind the wheel, and he is waving a weapon at her while cruising.

Not every department does high-risk stops the same way, so we make sure that new officers and those transferring are playing by the same page of the program, that they know our policy on the use of deadly force when stopping vehicles. When can you legally shoot? When can't you? As the situation is unfolding, the primary officer, the one who first saw the suspects, gives the instructions to cars who are assisting him. "I want your car here and this one set up back there," he says. "Here's where I want you to position yourself. Do this once we've made the stop."

We drill these skills into our people so they respond instinctively in positioning their car, taking cover, getting suspects out of their car and into their area of control. Raw intelligence is needed out on the street because the situation can change quickly. The bad guy doesn't know the script, so he improvises as he goes along.

I've been in law enforcement for twenty years, and the felony stops we make now are totally different than when I started. Police have done some wacky stops in the past and gotten killed doing it. Sometimes, changes in equipment help enormously: take our bright lights that can be beamed on a suspect's vehicle, making it harder for him to shoot at us. Our weapons have changed radically as well. We're using more semi-automatic weapons, and more officers now carry shotguns in their cars. The bad guys upgraded their weapons, and we had to match them.

We also strongly encourage our officers to wear soft body-protective clothing while out on the road. It saves lives! It's not exactly bulletproof, and it won't stop rifle fire, but it is bullet resistant and will stop certain projectiles. It's made of Kevlar, plus a metal shock plate.

The street battle is always escalating. Just like with firearms, some of the crooks are already wearing soft body armor. But the guy who's sporting it isn't your typical papa, who gets drunk, beats up mamma, and then drives around town waving a gun. It's the crook who's carefully planning to knock off a bank or who's bringing in cocaine under the back seat of his Volvo. And, unfortunately, he'll be the occupant you'll encounter in your next high-risk vehicle stop.

Illegal Immigrants

El Paso, Texas

"I think we have a good attitude toward them. They know we're just doing our jobs. If they get nabbed, they know we're gonna turn 'em over to the border patrol. And if they get collared inside a business or a residence, well, that's it for them. They're arrested and jailed."

"Often the human cost of these illegal entries is high. People fall from trains or suffocate in closed boxcars. There are all those drownings and the fights. And countless people get nailed crossing the highways."

Some cross the border in vehicles. Others swim or walk, depending on the water's height. It's just one great flow of immigrants, with the majority of them being Mexican. Most are looking for jobs, but a small percentage are criminals. They cross the border to commit burglaries and thefts and to sell drugs. They're the ones who make the honest aliens look bad.

We don't just stop them and check for citizenship. That's the responsibility of the U.S. Border Patrol. Our procedures are pretty straightforward: if they commit a crime, we arrest them, just like anyone else. Once they're let go and sent back to Mexico, they usually cross back over again. It's just a merry-go-round-and-round, back and forth!

Lots of accidents and injuries occur in the border crossings into the United States. Some drown in the Rio Grande. Others get hit by the trains while crossing the tracks, or they're run over by cars as they cross the highways. Once there's an injury or a fatality, it's our case, our jurisdiction.

I sympathize with these people. You know, it's so hard for them to live. The economy of Mexico is so bad, and they're really trying to make the best of it. Most of them are honest, hardworking citizens and they come here looking for a job. They want to become U.S. citizens just like you or me. I don't mind them being here as long as they aren't doing any harm.

The Mexican authorities cooperate with us a lot. If we're chasing somebody and we know we're gonna lose him once he's crossed back over, we'll advise them by radio, and they'll get on to him.

We run into all sorts of abuse out here, but we usually ignore it. Most of it won't hurt us; it's just verbal stuff. I really can't remember an incident where I've felt in real physical danger from illegal immigrants, though danger's always just below the surface. And there've been cases where an officer has been hurt in a scuffle when some of them are resisting arrest.

If these illegal immigrants have a favorite crime, it's got to be burglary. They knock off apartments, houses, cars — it doesn't matter. There's a little shoplifting and occasional vandalism as well. And you have to move fast if you think you're going to catch them. We've lost quite a few suspects because they're so quick. They bust a window and grab the goods, and in less than a minute they're over on the other side and safely in Mexico. That's how close we are to the border here. No delays at the border. No clearing of customs. They just run into the river and back to their own country with the stolen merchandise. So much of this has been going on that if a person is robbed or assaulted, first thing we do is try to cut the criminal off at the border. It doesn't always work, naturally.

I don't mind those immigrants who cross over to go to work. It's the ones who come here to commit crimes. They're the ones that really bother me. And businessmen in the area feel the same way. All we do is book them. A few days later, they're back again making trouble.

Many illegal immigrants get into the United States by crossing the river. One guy was ingenious and charged two dollars a head to float people across on an inflatable rubber duckie. Lots of them are skittish around water or just don't want to get wet. Many of them underestimate the current and misjudge its strength. Some have lost their lives to it. We responded to one incident not long ago where two youths were floating across on a pipe of some sort during high winds. They lost their balance and fell in the water. One of them made it, but the other one's body was found two miles south of where he fell in.

Sometimes it's no better for them on dry land. We had an incident last week just like that one several years ago where the aliens were being illegally smuggled inside railroad boxcars. It wasn't too far from here, only there were about six of them this time. According to the newspaper, the boxcar wasn't as vacuum-packed as the one where those eigh-

Peter Hendrie

Peter Hendrie

"I sympathize with these people. You know, it's so hard for them to live. The economy of Mexico is so bad, and they're really trying to make the best of it. They want to become U.S. citizens just like you or me."

teen passed away. These six were able to cut holes in the boxcar to get some air.

Lots of times we'll have crooked immigrants assaulting others. It's not really a gang-related thing. It's just a few individuals who take what little money these poor souls are carrying.

I'm not the least overwhelmed by the border crossings and what I see down here. Really! I've lived here all my life, so I'm used to these illegal crossovers. And I'm not sure there's much more that can be done about it. The border patrol is picking them up as best it can, and we grab them once a crime's been committed. We try to put them away as long as possible, but the way the system operates, they're out fast. Some of them know their rights better than we do. I don't know whether it's because they've read about them or because they've been picked up so many times that they know the arrest and interviewing procedures by heart.

Speaking Spanish really helps. You can talk honestly with them and keep up with the ones who try to lie to you. We always try to deal with them as people. If they get assaulted, even though they're illegal immigrants, we treat them the same as a U.S. citizen. If they need medical attention, we'll give it to them. If they are assaulted, we'll apprehend the individual that did them wrong.

■

What was a trickle of people a few years ago, is getting to be a cascade. Most of the aliens are just trying to find decent work in El Paso or are passing through to some other western U.S. state. Those are the ones who are looking for a train, a bus, a plane, or they're just walking to their destination.

I think we have a good attitude toward them. They know we're just doing our jobs. If they get nabbed, they know we're gonna turn 'em over to the border patrol. And if they get collared inside a business or a residence, well, that's it for them. They're arrested and jailed. We have a good understanding about this. And we usually get a suspect sooner or later. They might be lucky and get back south across the border. But they always, always, come back again. We might hear it through the grapevine, and we'll just go out of our way to greet them.

We have a liaison with the Mexican authorities in Juarez. He's the one in charge of communicating with the Mexican government. If something happens, we'll exchange information. If it's real important, like aggravated robbery or homicide, we'll call a dispatcher and meet the Mexican authorities at the middle of the bridge. It can be like High Noon out there — an international get-together midway, a kind of international bonding.

Over the last ten years there's been a large influx of real poor people from the interior of Mexico coming into Juarez. They work there for maybe six months to a year and then realize it's not all that profitable. Twenty or twenty-five dollars a week is not very much money. They can't go home, because it's only worse there, so they stay in Juarez and take up alternative work, which is coming over here to El Paso to commit crimes. I'd guess 10 to 15 percent of crimes around here are committed by illegal aliens, maybe as much as 35 percent in some categories. If we didn't have them, El Paso's crime rate would be a lot lower compared to other cities in the state of Texas or in the nation.

■

There are many ways to make a buck off an alien. Some guys get a dollar or so to carry them across the river in their arms or in small rafts. At night, gangs hang out on the other side and prey on the aliens. They make them pay a toll — two or three dollars each — just to cross the river. If they don't fork up the money, they risk being beaten up or even shot at while they're midstream. Once the sun comes up, that stuff stops. The border patrol is out and about by then, or maybe we'll get the word and we'll be there.

But if you were to walk out in the dark a short distance from the river, you'd definitely get robbed, you'd most likely get mugged, and

you might even get killed. Even some of the streets around here, the ones with two or three bars, are just full of no-accounts. Anything can happen. We've had our share of murders down there and at least two or three robberies a night. It's a happening place — complete with illegal alien prostitutes and illegal alien transvestites — right up until about four or five o'clock in the morning.

Come six o'clock and you'll be able to see the morning stream of immigrants on the Black Bridge out beyond the river levee. That's where trains cross over from Mexico, and it's a handy entrance for aliens who don't want to pay any money to get in. All they do is run across the bridge and climb a gate that's about twelve feet high. They bring their own makeshift ladders. One guy holds it, and the others scurry up and over. Once they hit American soil, they run this way and that, looking all about to see if any border patrolmen are around. They're not afraid of us, because they know that the police can't get involved. Once in the clear, they just mingle with the people. Most of them will return to their homes in Mexico come evening. The funny thing is that a lot of these people could get a permit to enter the country legally for a day or two. It allows them to cross over, buy items, do whatever they want to do, and then go back. But most find it easier to take the chance of getting caught entering illegally rather than the hassle and cost of getting the permit.

But often the human cost of these illegal entries is high. People fall from trains or suffocate in closed boxcars. There are all those drownings and the fights. And countless people get nailed crossing the highways. One transvestite got run over last night crossing one of the roads. She or he, or whatever, got hit by a truck, and everything flew, the high heels, the wig, everything! The person will likely die from the injuries. It was a big surprise. He was taken to the hospital, and everyone thought he was a female, until they started taking off all his clothes.

El Paso County provides all the emergency services when aliens get injured. We don't just transport them to the middle of the bridge and hand 'em over to another ambulance. We take them to the county hospital, and we'll care for them as long as needed, regardless if they have money or not. We give them several months to come up with it, and if they don't, then, unfortunately, they're guests of the county of El Paso, which ends up footing the bill.

There used to be a lot of exploitation of the medical system, particularly in terms of childbirths. Pregnant women would cross over in the midst of labor pains. We'd really have no option but take them to the county hospital. A little more than 50 percent of them would end up paying for the services rendered, but that was when the immigration laws were different. It used to be that when a child was born in the United States, both he and his parents got preference in emigrating to this country. The law now only gives preferential treatment to the child, so it's no longer a free ticket into the United States for the folks.

Pedal Patrol

Casper, Wyoming

"People don't really believe I'm a cop until the second glance. It's the informality. In shorts and on a bike, how can that be a police officer? Hopefully, this will work to our advantage against criminals. We'll take them by surprise!"

Peter Hendrie

"I've written a lot of traffic tickets from the bike, and, amazingly enough, cars actually stop… You pedal real fast after them, get up close, and wave 'em down. We've toyed with the idea of adding a siren, but the bike's really not an emergency vehicle."

We wheeled out the pedal patrol in response to complaints from town merchants. They were fed up with all the public drinking and wild skateboarders who were rolling into pedestrians downtown. The community imposed a set of new ordinances to confront the problem, and we decided the best way to uphold them was to up the ante against these offenders. If our officers had to chase around kids with high-technology skateboards, then we'd use an even better technology to pursue them — mountain bikes!

The pedal patrol has been a big success. Having an officer patrol on his mountain bike enables him to get around fast and be highly visible. The skateboard problem has pretty much vanished. Shopkeepers now wave at the pedal patrol as it rolls by. It makes us look more modern and in touch, particularly among the hard-core bike enthusiasts. The public relations value has been great.

Prior to instituting the pedal patrol, vandalism was a real problem. Planting and the general landscape downtown was being trampled and destroyed. Elderly people were particularly worried that they might be hurt. They demanded that the city council and the police do something about it. For our part, we wanted to avoid a bad police image. All we needed was for the public to see an officer rushing his patrol vehicle into the park, jumping out, and chasing children down the street! But the mountain bike does nothing to tarnish the police department image, and if the pedal patrol continues to be successful, we will probably expand it and pursue even tougher crimes. This is what the Seattle police have been doing successfully.

When an officer rides his bike into the park, it's a kind of deterrent to vandalism, fights, and drinking. It also dissuades the person who's thinking about breaking into a car or assaulting someone. Of course, the nice thing about the pedal patrol is its cost. We can outfit the officer for less than $1,500. Sure, the bike seems pricey, but not when parked next to a patrol car.

Peter Hendrie

The pedal patrol is just an offshoot of the old foot patrol. You're a little more mobile, but you're still close to the public. Our bike program was basically plagiarized from the Seattle Police Department.

I've written a lot of traffic tickets from the bike, and, amazingly enough, cars actually stop when you tell them to. You pedal real fast after them, get up close, and wave 'em down. We've toyed with the idea of adding a siren, but the bike's really not an emergency vehicle. People don't really believe I'm a cop until the second glance. It's the informality. In shorts and on a bike, how can that be a police officer? Hopefully, this will work to our advantage against criminals. We'll take them by surprise!

One big benefit of the pedal patrol is the physical exercise I get. Not only am I more fit, but when I come off the shift, I'm so relaxed, compared to when I used to get out of the patrol car so uptight. It's a great release. And with the mountain bike and a road bike I ride on my time off, I'm now traveling two hundred to three hundred miles a week. A cop who's a hundred pounds overweight might not be too happy on the pedal patrol, but anyone in decent shape is going to love it.

"When an officer rides his bike into the park, it's a kind of deterrent to vandalism, fights, and drinking. It also dissuades the person who's thinking about breaking into a car or assaulting someone… Sure, the bike seems pricey, but not when parked next to a patrol car."

Street Incidents

Tucson, Arizona

"I could do this job for the rest of my life. If I could do it when I was eighty, I would. I don't need any stripes; I don't need any bars. I just want to be out on the street. Lots of people say I'm nuts to put up with the shots, the screams, and the sirens. And they'd probably run from the stress as well."

It's sad how badly people treat each other. I saw this little old bag lady. There she was in the Greyhound Bus Depot, so fragile she couldn't hurt a fly, and along come a couple of whacked-out kids. They stole her purse and pummelled her with grapefruits. They literally ripped her purse off her shoulder, and she had to be hospitalized. You know what? Turns out she didn't even have any money in her purse. Not one damn cent! Just those crumpled-up tissues that old ladies carry.

Another time, two guys met one another at a homosexual bar, and to make a long story short, one of them chopped the ring finger off the other. A detective on the case called me to find a third party, named Eddie, who had introduced these two. This other guy was a transvestite, and I've got to tell you, a reserve officer who was with me fell in love with Eddie, he was so good-looking. He thought this was just the neatest looking girl he'd ever seen, until I informed him Eddie was a guy.

Anyway, we're out interviewing Eddie when this guy walks up to him and says, "Hey, Eddie, how's it goin'?" Well, I'd already asked Eddie if he knew the suspect, and he had said no. But I'm lookin' real hard at this guy, and I'm remembering the description. "What's your name?" He says he just got out of prison and refused to give his name. Right about then the sheriff's deputies arrived and arrested him. This guy was a dangerous fella. He'd gotten pissed off at his victim and had cut his finger off, real slow. Now that's the kinda guy you'd like to see put away.

At one point, we were experiencing a rash of robberies of convenience stores in the city. We'd have four or five of them in one part of town each night. They even shot and killed a couple of clerks in the robberies. In response we began staking out the convenience stores nightly. It lasted for eighteen solid months. It got so the department only let us take the lousy days of the week off — days like Tuesday and Wednesday, when the computer said the least number of robberies were likely to occur. The word eventually got out

"In some cities citizens seldom bother to call the cops. They think they'll write it down over the phone but do absolutely nothing about it. Not in Tucson! The community's more active here. If a garden hose was ripped off, they'd call for a patrol car."

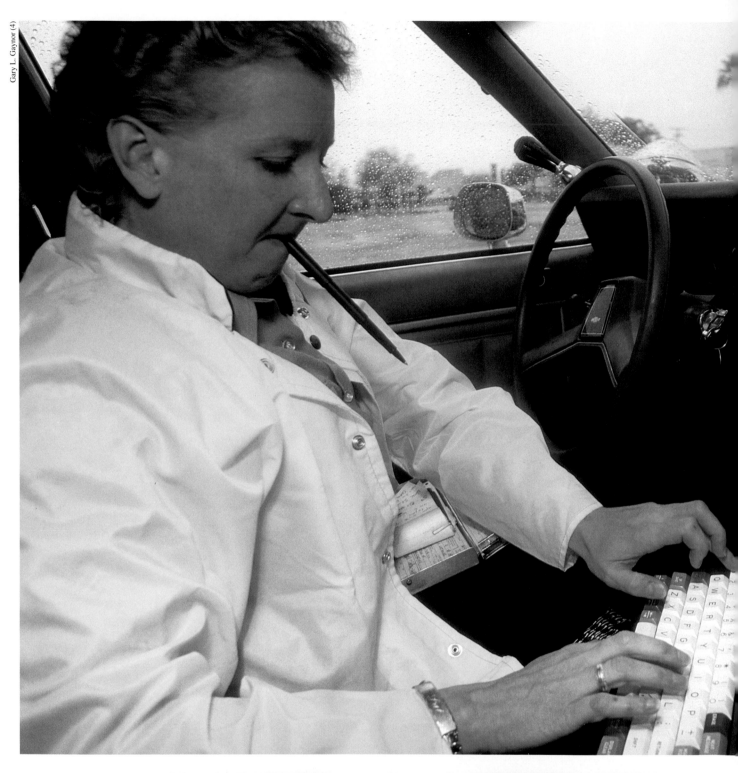

Gary L. Gaynor (4)

that we were there, and the robberies tapered off, but for a year and a half, it was stakeout, stakeout, stakeout.

It used to be a big week in this town if we got several hundred calls for assistance. Now you can't keep count. We're not like the big city where people just shrug, "What's a cop gonna do?" In some cities citizens seldom bother to call the cops. They think they'll write it down over the phone but do absolutely nothing about it. Not in Tucson! The community's more active here. If a garden hose was ripped off, they'd call for a patrol car.

I'm an old-timer on the force, and I feel our job is to help the rookies. I tell 'em, "If you've ever got a question, feel free to ask me, out on the street or wherever. I may not know the answer, but I'll sure as hell help you find someone who does. Or we'll go to the library and look it up." But they seem to be a new breed. Maybe it's the way they're getting trained, but they're just not talking to the old heads even though we're a natural resource. If you have twenty years on the street, you've learned something useful every single day.

Over the years my partner and I have made some good collars. If you're a good two-man team and have a good partner, someone you can really trust, that's the greatest. You don't see it often, and you hate like hell to lose it. But it's as predictable as baseball trades. Sooner or later you and your partner are going to be split up.

We've had some funny incidents for sure. I don't know if you wanna hear about the time we were looking down the street and about three hundred pounds of woman picked up her dress and, I swear to God, took a dump right on the corner. And you know what? We didn't have a law to cover it. At the time, the city code only covered urinating in public. That code changed real fast. But what were we to do? Get her for pollution?

Most holidays and weekends, we'd get several hundred locals down at this particular club. They'd be tanked up and dancing and frolicking. Eventually, somebody would start something, and the knives would come out. We'd have all kinds of stabbings, and many of them weren't with knives. The beer of choice at this club is a long-necked bottle of beer. Finally we figured it out. Take a longneck and crack it, and you've got yourself one serious weapon to shove in somebody's face. We've seen the Indians take off more than a few ears in the parking lot this way. One crazy guy became so upset at something one night that he cranked off a round with his twenty-two rifle directly into the sidewalk near us. We almost took him out then and there.

At Tenth Street and Fifth Avenue one time, we came across a little guy in the door of a lounge. He stared hard at us, and then real quick assumed a military stance and went for a gun in his shirt. I pushed my sidekick behind the car and hugged the corner of the building. I could just hear the click of the gun hammer hitting metal. At that moment, I wondered if I was down or what, it was all happening so fast. After a second, I peeked around the corner, my gun drawn. The guy's in the process of putting his own gun back in his shirt, and he's taking off around the corner. We chase after him, and when I finally got about six yards away from him, he started to bring out the gun again. Just then, I landed hard on top of him. I could've killed this guy justifiably then and there, but I didn't. After he was in custody, we discover there aren't any bullets in his weapon. Apparently, he was just angling to be killed by a cop. It must be his special way of committing suicide.

I'd quit smoking just before this happened — for three months, ninety-seven days, cold turkey! But, boy, did this get me started on 'em again quick. First cop I saw I said, "Gimme a cigarette," and I've been back every since. That was five or six years ago. I'm getting to the point now where I say to myself, "Why are you still here? Why are you still alive?" I could've been killed in this job at any time. That's maybe why I don't like to bring it up or talk about it a lot. I'm just like the guy who's been in Vietnam or Korea or World War II.

You had to know how to work the bars. If you didn't, then you had a lot of problems. We might enter a place any time between six at night and one-fifteen in the morning, when they close. We never had a routine where they could predict we'd pass by every fifteen or twenty minutes. We never let them know the sequence in which we'd visit different bars. They might not see us for an hour because we'd taken someone to jail. After a while you get to know the troublemakers. If one was really getting out of hand, we'd cut him off in every bar around. We'd literally tell all the bar owners, the guy's had enough to drink, and if he walked into their establishment, we were going to arrest him. A lot of times, we've been able to keep a lid on things this way.

Girls were sometimes the ones who created the biggest problems. They'd get in major brawls! The hair would be flying everywhere and you'd have five hundred pounds of women just rolling all over the place. Here you are, trying desperately to wedge them apart. You don't want to hurt 'em. You don't want to get crushed to death. And most of all, you don't want the bar to be chanting "police brutality." All you're trying to do is to pry 'em loose and send 'em home in different directions. It's a situation that can quickly escalate into a little miniriot if you don't know what you're doing.

Just booking a prisoner can sometimes be the biggest threat to safety on the streets! We'll collar a felon on a busy bar night. Rather than taking the criminal to jail ourselves, we'll try to get a separate unit to come by and run the garbage out. One night, near closing time for the bars, we asked for a delivery unit to take our prisoner to lockup, but the sergeant wouldn't let us have it. We decided to make a little point.

It was Saturday night, shortly after twelve o'clock. We made a misdemeanor arrest, and, by God, we transported him ourselves. Well, it sometimes takes an hour or two to book a prisoner into jail. On a Saturday night, quite a few cops are lined up booking their catches. So there we are sitting at the air-conditioned jail, waiting our turn. One o'clock comes and goes. The clock ticks on. I turn on the handy talkie and hear car after car being dispatched. Officers are screaming for backup in that area where we normally prevent a lot of shit from happening. Fights have broken out here and there.

That sergeant came up to me the next night and asks, "Where were you guys?" and I respond, "We made an arrest; we were at the jail." "Did you have to make that arrest just after midnight?" he asked. I said, "Well, yeah. You were the one that told us we had to transport our own prisoners." He then looks at me and says, "I think I'm getting your drift." After that we got transport for our prisoners whenever we needed it.

Lots of people used to say, "How can that be fun being a cop working those bars?" You're going from bar to bar sweeping out a junkie here and an armed robber there. It's a menagerie of crime, populated by pimps, hookers, rapists and murderers — all the folks you probably don't want in your own neighborhood. Well, our job is to keep those in the menagerie in and all the others out. For example, you've got the tourists from all over the world. These crazy tourists! They'd come in here and want to go to a certain club. And they'd ask, "Officer, is it all right to go in there and have a drink?" I'd steer 'em clear fast and say, "If you value your personal safety, perhaps the Holiday Inn bar is a little better for you." That probably happened a million times over the years.

A bulldozer in a couple of days finally did what we couldn't in twenty years. It turned the strip into a burial ground for our many headaches. Now those clubs are just parking lots and offices.

But getting rid of the bars didn't get rid of the guys who commit the crimes. For example, one day I was just walking the beat, twirling my baton, and came across one of them I knew by sight. He was holding a woman down on the ground. He was literally on top of her, his hands at her throat. She was screaming so wildly the whole neighborhood could hear. Her Levi's had been unbuttoned, and he was attempting to rape her. I brought out my weapon and began pulling the man off. When he looked up in astonishment, and saw the barrel of my .357 magnum, he took off

fast. I've got to tell you, there's no greater feeling than coming along at the right moment and, perhaps, saving someone's life.

After I'd calmed the lady and someone was caring for her, I got on the air to call for help and then took off in pursuit. In the meantime, the suspect, at a dead run, had crashed head-on into an attorney down the street a bit. This lawyer knew the guy as well and just sensed that something bad was going down. He grabbed him and said, "Hold on, now. Why don't we just have a chat with the police." The kid kept struggling to get away, so the lawyer laid one right on his jaw.

I've got a lot of praise for that lawyer. If anybody should get a commendation, it should be him. He didn't know if the suspect was going to pull one of those Crocodile Dundee knives, or a pistol, for that matter. He took a helluva chance. And got a good one in, too. About the time he punched him, I saw it from a distance and slowed down my arrival, you know, kinda hoping maybe he'd get a couple more good shots in. A civilian can do things we just can't.

For me, the incident was a welcome break these days. Most of the time, I'm keeping an eye on the transients, the senior citizens, and the commuters going to work downtown. It's mainly dealing with misdemeanors for drinking in public, parking violations, and exciting stuff like that, so when you actually break up a rape in progress, it just makes the job worthwhile.

How things change! Nineteen years ago, when I became a cop, it was okay to shoot a felon who tried to flee a crime. Take the guy in this rape incident. He's just hopping off the girl and starting to run. Not so many years ago, I could have easily capped one off — and gotten away with it! But no longer. The rules have changed, and I have to be thinking to myself, "He's not a direct threat to her. He's not armed, and he's certainly no threat to me." Even so, I get this passing feeling of wanting to shoot him. When you've got daughters, like I do, and even though you've been raised a Catholic, you think, "Maybe I should've just brought his life to an end right there, just to get him off the street." It would be different if you knew the judicial system worked. Then this guy would get what he deserves, even if it were only the proper mental help. He's done it before, and he'll likely do it again once the courts let him out.

Downtown used to be on the dark side, with a few blocks that attracted a kind of client you wouldn't see in a nice place. Many of them would leave the bars drunk and get rolled in the alleys. We used to spend a lot of time dealing with this. We still have a big transient problem, unfortunately. A lot of them are there by choice. It's their way of life. A lot of times people don't want to hear the truth. All you hear is "Help the homeless! Help the homeless!" But if you went to the Salvation Army with me at mealtime, I think you could easily pick out the small percentage that are truly homeless and those who are just bums. We're always going to have this situation. In the winter, many of them come down from states where it's cold. They winter here! They'll be "bleeding," you know, giving blood to get their nickle and dime bags of marijuana. They've got enough for wine and beer. And they get fed three times a day for free.

Concern for the safety of the senior citizens grew in 1985 when a seventy-four-year-old man was bludgeoned to death by a transient after a fight broke out while free cheese was being handed out at the recreation center. And just recently, not far from here, a drunk transient killed another one. For what? Four crummy dollars to go get a cheap jug of wine. There's a blood bank just west of the recreation center and temporary housing near there, so homeless are constantly moving through the area. The transients are panhandling, and it's getting to the point of outright extortion. Twenty years ago they were called hobos, and they'd say, "Hey, could you spare a guy a dime?" Now they're the homeless, and many of them are saying, "Gimme a dollar or else!" Say that to some seventy-, eighty-, or ninety-year-old senior citizens and it's gonna scare the hell out of them.

Now we give these oldsters a lot more attention, and they're very, very appreciative, *very* appreciative. That's the self-gratification, the self-satisfaction, that keeps me going as a policeman. It makes me really enjoy puttin' on that uniform, and I look forward to comin' to work. I could do this job for the rest of my life. If I could do it when I was eighty, I would. I don't need any stripes; I don't need any bars. I just want to be out on the street. Lots of people say I'm nuts to put up with the shots, the screams, and the sirens. And they'd probably run the other way from the stress as well. Normal people probably think policemen who love their jobs are a little off or something.

But, without a doubt, if I had it to do over again, I wouldn't have gotten married before starting the job. That's about the only thing I would've changed. I would have ultimately married the same woman, but first gimme about three or four years of single life on the beat, because, boy, do you meet some good-lookin' women. Man! It's easy to be an adulterer out there!

My dad was a cop for twenty-five years. Watching and listening to him helped my career. He taught me to treat people with respect, regardless of how they look — even if they're a little grimy or have dirt under their fingernails. A person could be just down on his luck. He might even be a rapist, a robber, or a murderer. But when you make that initial contact, you've got to give him the benefit of the doubt. Do it until the point where he disrespects you, starts shooting off or giving you probable cause. I've gotten along real well with that philosophy. But it doesn't hurt to be six-foot-six and 280 pounds, either.

Domestic Violence

Boise, Idaho

"Alcohol or drugs are involved in virtually all domestic violence. That's especially true during major holidays, when everybody seems to be partying. All of the stress seems to take its toll on couples. One or both of them inevitably start drinking heavily, and, whammo, they're blaming each other for everything bad in their lives."

Responding to a domestic dispute has its element of danger. The battling couple instinctively forms a bond upon our arrival, and their anger gets turned on us. But I suppose it's better to have them mad at us than at each other. We're equipped to deal with it.

It's usually a no-win situation. I may arrest a husband or wife, and then the other partner decides not to prosecute when it comes to court. If there are no witnesses, that too, can be a big problem. Winning or losing the case may depend upon proving that someone is lying.

Some calls are particularly tense, especially the ones where you've just told the husband he has to leave the house, and he's distraught and darts out the door as if he's going for a weapon. You go after him and try to keep things under control. But everything's in complete turmoil, with lots of yelling and screaming and the kids in tears. You enter such situations in fear, but you're well trained to stay calm, and objectively you do the job you're there to do.

Alcohol or drugs are involved in virtually all domestic violence. That's especially true during Christmas, New Year's Eve, and the other major holidays, when everybody seems to be partying. All of the stress of those big holidays seems to take its toll on couples. One or both of them inevitably start drinking heavily, and, whammo, they're blaming each other for everything bad in their lives.

The parents are lucky. They have options. They can fight and go their own way. But the real victims are the kids. They have none. They have to sit there and witness or experience the abuse. Just like in a divorce, the separation of a couple because of domestic violence affects the children the most. The kids usually love both parents, and it's shattering to see one of them hauled off to jail. For us, as police officers, to talk to the kids at the time of the arrests doesn't do much good, because the emotions of the youngsters are so high. They need to come down from that highly emotional state before we can deal with their problems.

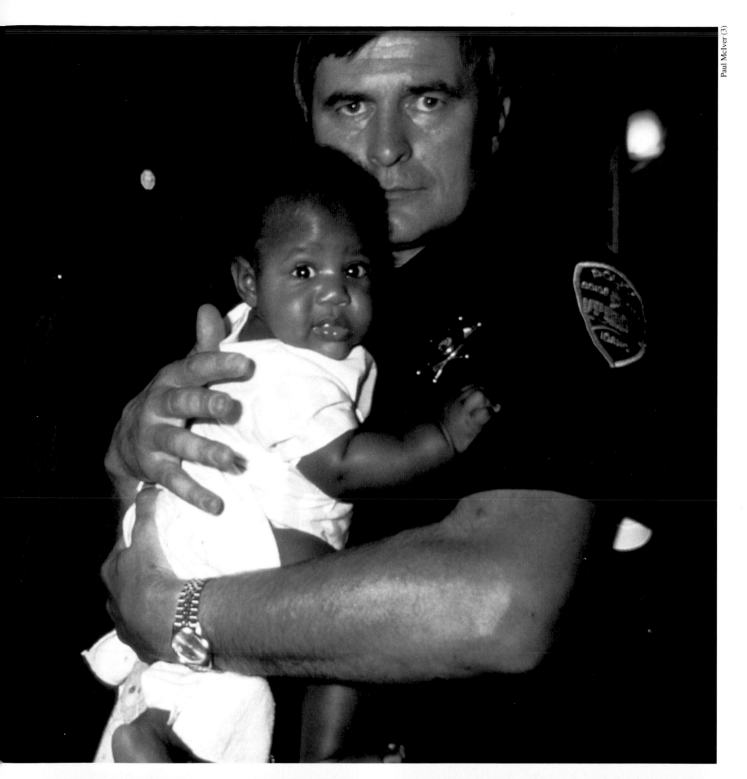

I find that abuse of children occurs at levels from the poorest to the wealthiest families. Also, the problem runs the gamut from neglect of the child to actual physical abuse.

There is more pressure on parents today and consequently on the children. Parents pressure kids to excel in sports, music, schoolwork, and just about everything. The parents are all stressed out just trying to achieve a little financial success. In the last three months alone I've had half a dozen kids tell me they want to move out of their homes. It seldom happened before — fifteen- or sixteen-year-old kids wanting to move out. Some of them had been physically or emotionally abused. I've talked to the parents, and they say, "Yes, we did that and we're sorry and we won't do it again." But too often they do.

■

Kids are the real losers in most domestic violence cases. We had one situation the other day involving a family of four. The man was not the natural father of the children, but was the woman's fiancé. He had his own home. These kids were just darling, but when we got to the house, they were cowering behind their mom. I felt very sorry for them and wondered what kind of life they were going to have in an environment like this. I don't feel particularly sorry for the mom. She'll just continue her drinking. We separated the man and woman for the night, but she kept coming out and saying "Well, he can stay if he wants." And we'd say, "No, he should be out of here, at least for the time being." The worst thing was the two kids, who were just looking on at all this. These youngsters were probably in some danger, but the law doesn't allow us to take them out of the house unless the danger's imminent. Mom being drunk doesn't count. In the end, I couldn't make an arrest, because nobody would admit that violence had occurred. I left the place feeling sick and helpless.

After stuff like this, it's hard to get the job out of your head. Driving home, you're still the police officer, constantly looking around and checking things out. It's hard to

get off duty, psychologically. I like to make time to go camping far up in the mountains. You don't have to see anybody there, or worry about crime or get involved in these emotional struggles. That's the way I cope with this job — just head for the mountains and go fishing.

Police life intrudes on my social life on every level. There are not a lot of us women in law enforcement. And most of my friends work nine-to-five jobs. I normally have the graveyard shifts and weekend duty, which is when others aren't working. I don't feel like I've lost friends, but it's just that I don't associate with them very much and I feel like I'm not invited to so many parties anymore. After all, who wants a cop around? I end up spending a lot of time with my immediate family. I don't think my husband would like it so much if I said, "I'm going out with the guys from the police department." Yes, being a female cop affects your social life, but I wouldn't want to trade jobs with anyone.

I've talked to a lot of people who beat their spouses. To them, having their wives removed to a shelter home is like losing their last possession. It's a real psychological defeat. All they're left with is perhaps a job, their alcoholism, or whatever, and it's scary. It's the last straw.

I don't worry about getting hit trying to break them up — bruises heal. But if they go overboard and get a knife or a gun and grab onto her or a fellow officer, then I worry. We have to anticipate it to prevent it. The bizarre part of it is that they would rather hurt you, and badly if necessary, than suffer the embarrassment of getting arrested in front of their family. In these situations, I'm extremely concerned about my own safety and the safety of my partner because these people often act so irrationally. You have to step back from the situation for a minute to calm them down and try to get some rational thinking going. And when substance abuse is involved, that's a difficult task.

The other night, we got a call from a little six-year-old girl who had run to the convenience store to report a man with a knife at a family fight. One of the people at the house had been cut, but we didn't know which one. The first thing we did, even before going into the house, was meet with the girl. We prefer to act cautiously and carefully. That's what we're trained to do.

When we got to the house, it was typical! They were both intoxicated. He had a knife wound, but said he had cut himself with a pair of scissors. She wouldn't admit to anything: "Not me, I wasn't hit. Whatever made you think that?" Neither of them wanted us in the house, and we didn't have any criminal violation because no one was admitting anything.

I asked the kids whether they'd seen anything. They said no. Kids get real scared in these situations. Most of the time they claim to have seen nothing. One of the kids said his dad cut himself with a screwdriver while fixing his bike. And dad's saying he cut himself with a pair of scissors. So you've got injuries, but nobody's saying how it happened. So we can't make a probable cause arrest on a domestic battery charge, because maybe one happened, and then again, maybe one didn't. The facts and probable cause just weren't there. If he had said, "She cut me with a knife," we would have some evidence, seized the knife, and probably made an arrest. But when everybody's denying it and not wanting us there and the guy's really loaded, it's impossible. Even now, we still don't know if he cut himself, if she did it, or what happened exactly.

When I go out on a call, I get basic information from the parties. I question all of them in an attempt to assess the situation. If a woman appears to have been assaulted, but is denying it, I'll ask her whether there's a prior history of battery in their family. She might say, "All I know is his dad's an alcoholic, and he beat up on his mom." At that point, I try to get her to talk some more about their problems and try to identify any psychological baggage they may be carrying. I would try to get her to admit that there is a serious problem and that someone needs help. I'd try to persuade her to file charges, if appropriate, so that the man is forced by the courts to get some counseling.

Usually, with a first-time offense, if the assault isn't too severe, the guy will get a suspended jail sentence, but will be required to go into counseling.

■

Society needs to break the cycle of spouses beating up on each other. It seems like there are a lot more cases of such domestic violence than when I started on the job three years ago, and they're more severe. Incidents are not limited to just the lower socioeconomic level. We've arrested attorneys and other professional people. We get men who attack their wives, and females who attack their husbands — it works both ways. Increasingly it's younger couples. They live together or get married, and it's a lark at first, but then they find that they're not really committed to the relationship. For whatever reason, they just start picking away at each other, and it gets more and more vicious.

We respond to such incidents differently than we did in the old days. Years ago, the officers would ask the aggressive participant to leave the room. We'd talk the problem out with them rather than arrest anyone. Now our stance is pro-arrest — get the violator out of there and get him treatment.

Recently the state of Idaho enacted a new law, whereby victims of domestic violence can seek a protective restraining order from the courts. The order requires that if a man or a woman has a recent history of violent behavior toward the spouse or companion, the threatening person must move from the residence. For a specified number of days, there can be no contact with the other party — no letters, no phone calls, and no going near the workplace. When that law was enacted last July, we did extensive training to prepare our officers to enforce it fairly. We wanted them to be sensitive to the problems people face and to know how to deal with the hostilities that can arise.

In the past, officers felt that they should do very little at the scene of domestic disputes. We assumed the abused person must be basi-

Peter Hendrie

"Police life intrudes on my social life on every level… I don't feel like I've lost friends, but it's just that I don't associate with them very much and I feel like I'm not invited to so many parties anymore. After all, who wants a cop around?… Yes, being a female cop affects your social life, but I wouldn't want to trade jobs with anyone."

cally happy in their situation or else he or she would leave. Why stay and take a pounding on a regular basis? But if you look at it more closely, just what options are really available? How will you support yourself or see that the kids are cared for? There are many obligations and responsibilities that tie abused people to their abusers. These are the realities we try to train our officers to recognize when they arrive on the scene.

When officers arrive at the scene of a domestic disturbance, and can see that someone has been assaulted, we immediately try to help the victim. Usually, tempers are still high when we arrive. The hostility tends to turn away from the people who are fighting each other toward us. "Who called you? What are you doing on my property?" If we see evidence of a clear violation, we arrest the person immediately. Some women who actually want their husbands out of there have difficulty saying, "I want this man arrested," because the hostility immediately turns from the officer back on them. Often the man will say, "If you don't drop that charge, I am going to beat you unmercifully." Lots of fear is at play. So by making an arrest and jailing him, the heat's off her. We don't mind being tagged the bad guy in such a situation. The law exists, the guy's violated it, lock him up, no ifs, ands, or buts.

The costs of domestic violence to the community are considerable. The taxpayer pays for law enforcement and court costs. They pay police officers to referee family altercations. It's costly for the victim, who can have substantial medical bills. The shelter homes cost money as well. There are also the emotional costs, which can be the most expensive of all, not only for the battered adult, but for the kid who grows up thinking it's normal for a dad to beat up on a mom. And the effects are long-lasting. We're seeing a new generation of domestic disputes where the children of families I had to arrest or cool down years before have grown up and are having their own family fights.

In my estimation, the community has a larger role to play in curbing domestic violence. Society has responsibilities to fulfill.

The news media have focused attention on wife-beating incidents to sensitize the public. And we're working with a special committee on the problem, so that a person who's been convicted of such a crime is required to seek counseling. Look, it's not enough to just send a guy to jail, where he spends a little easy time, or to let him meet bail, with the judge saying, "Okay, mister, don't do it again." This does next to nothing about the underlying problem. Prevention and treatment must dovetail with the enforcement effort.

Take some of the violence off of TV, that might help. The community needs to be sensitive to domestic violence and the horror of people going at each other. On TV, it's an accepted practice — particularly on some soap operas and police and detective shows. How many times on TV do you see a person who's been arrested submit peacefully? Rarely! There's usually the big knockdown fight. Well, reality's become the imitation of what's on the tube! Try to arrest somebody now, and you won't be hearing, "Please, officer, cuff me, and I'll go along peacefully." More likely, they'll say, "No way! I'm not about to let some cop arrest me in my own living room without a fight." Society is mentally geared to this kind of thing by the one-eyed monster sitting in the corner of the room. It's becoming more and more desensitized to violent acts. Many of society's problems — and domestic violence is one of them — start in the home. That is where it must end. If that entails a Boise police officer's coming into the home to arrest a batterer in a domestic violence case, then so be it. We will do our part.

Prostitution

Las Vegas, Nevada

"Prostitution isn't just
two consenting adults
engaging in sex. People
inevitably get ripped off,
and drugs are usually
involved… Prostitution
costs the community
quite a bit… and the
money the city and the
county lost will never
be recouped."

"Every city in the world has prostitution to some degree. It might be open, or it might be out of sight, but, for sure, it's there!... Things seem to have changed quite a bit since the new sheriff got in... We've pretty much gotten the girls off the street. All of the other kinds of crimes that are related to prostitution have dropped as well."

Great big letters are emblazoned on the door of this downtown club. They scream out, "Prostitution is illegal!" But go in there, and sooner or later some girl will sidle up and ask you to pay fifty bucks to step in the back where, "we'll party naked." Does this constitute prostitution? Not by state law, but who are you kidding. People are being propositioned in there, sure as shootin'. That's prostitution going on behind those closed doors.

Out on the street, we're able to keep an eye on the action. Inside, it's a lot easier for them to slip things past us. When someone gets ripped off in one of these joints, they usually won't come forward. And ripped off they are! Fifty dollars is just the cover charge. Get inside and you're bilked much more. It may cost as much as three hundred to five hundred bucks. You'll probably leave so outraged that you want to file a crime report, but you won't, because you don't want your wife, your girlfriend, or mom and dad to know where you've been hanging out.

The situation used to be really terrible around here. Working graveyard on Las Vegas Boulevard, we'd just roll down the Strip hauling in the prostitutes. We'd get about 150 girls on an average weekend night.

The hookers would be taken to jail, given a citation, and released an hour or two later. It wasn't uncommon for us to drop 'em off at jail, and before we'd get past Fremont Street, they'd be back on the street.

Heavier penalties ultimately helped solve the problem on the streets. Instead of just waltzing in and out of the system, the prostitutes got hit with stiffer fines. The judges and the courts helped us on this.

Now few pimps are seen on the streets. Sometimes they're in the hotels, working as bellhops and elevator operators, or they're cab drivers. It's business as usual, and some hotels condone it. Plainclothes vice officers work all the hotels, and they've been doing a real good job even though they're understaffed.

Prostitution isn't just two consenting adults engaging in sex. People inevitably get ripped off, and drugs are usually involved.

Las Vegas has gotten a black eye from the image of prostitutes. I can't recall how many times a nice, average middle-aged couple from middle America would come up and say, "Hey, these three girls just asked my wife and me if we wanted to have group sex with them." Say that to a middle-aged woman from midriff America and she's likely to drop in her tracks!

The girls seem to come from all socio-economic groups and many from broken homes. Many have been abused sexually in the past. To them, sex is just a job — it means next to nothing. They work eight to ten hours a day giving pleasure to people who work eight to ten hours a day in their own jobs. In turn, we work eight to ten hours a day just to try to stop them.

It's not unusual to find out that one of these girls isn't really a girl at all. And it can be pretty disturbing for a guy to discover that the prostitute he's taken a shine to is really a man in female dress. Sometimes he'll react like his manhood's been insulted, and a fight breaks out. Some of the men who dress as female prostitutes can look spectacular. I had one I was booking one night and a highway patrol officer came up and said, "God, she's good-looking!" I responded, "Well, go say hi to her." They chatted for some time, and as I left the jail, I said, "Well, I hope you two guys have a nice time." I don't think the officer ever quite caught on.

AIDS is the most threatening aspect of prostitution today. In Las Vegas, right now, there are more than twenty known AIDS-carrying prostitutes working the streets. The john who decides to have a secret swing in Las Vegas doesn't really know the dimensions of the problem he's getting into. He returns home and infects his wife or friend with it. We've now got a felony charge on the books on AIDS. Once a prostitute is picked up for soliciting, she must take a blood test. If she's diagnosed as a carrier and she's picked up again, she's slapped with a felony. Until that time, the AIDS-carrier prostitute is basically walking the streets slowly killing people off.

Prostitution costs the community quite a bit, even when measured in terms of one victim. Let's say a prostitute picks the pocket of some john. He has several credit cards in the wallet she lifted. Each stolen card is going to be worth about $1,600 on the street. If the prostitute steals credit cards every day, that's going to add up to tens of thousands of dollars annually. Once the guy with the stolen wallet gets home, he'll tell his buddies, "Avoid Las Vegas! The place is out of control, and everybody's getting ripped off." Presto! Vegas ends up economically mugged. This stuff about prostitution being a victimless crime is a myth. It gave the city and the police department a black eye, and the money the city and the county lost will never be recouped.

But, you know, every city in the world has prostitution to some degree. It might be open, or it might be out of sight, but, for sure, it's there! Here we have the added attraction of gambling, which seems to go hand in hand with women. Things seem to have changed quite a bit since the new sheriff got in. Back in '83, when he started cleaning things up, we made more than twelve thousand arrests for prostitution. This year, I think, it's around twenty-five hundred, which shows that we've pretty much gotten the girls off the street. All of the other kinds of crimes that are related to prostitution have dropped as well. In fact, Las Vegas's rank as an American crime city has dropped from fifth in 1982 to around one hundred thirtieth today.

■

Prostitution is a direct kind of exploitation. We sometimes call it white slavery. We'd get these fresh-faced sixteen- or seventeen-year-old kids who'd age fifteen years overnight in the clutches of ruthless pimps and other characters who are out there exploiting them.

One pimp came home to find the prostitute who was living with him asleep in bed. He told her she should be out on the street working. And she gave him a little lip over that idea. So what does this guy do? He goes to the stove and heats up a pan of water. When it's boiling, he rips back the bed sheets

and throws it all over the girl's naked body. Second- and third-degree burns all over!

Basically, the pimp is society's parasite. He extorts by force or by threat to get a prostitute to do what he wants. Then he lives directly off her. Unfortunately, through intimidation of these girls, the pimp ends up making all their decisions.

A good percentage of prostitutes are addicted to drugs. It's almost like there's an inward progression once a girl's decided on a life of prostitution. The quality of life just isn't there! Her world becomes one of mental anguish. Too confused to really remember the past or to envision the future. Drugs become increasingly necessary just for her to escape her reality.

Before the current administration in Las Vegas, prostitution was getting so bad on the Strip that girls would literally walk up to cars at red lights, lean in, and proposition the drivers. While doing that, they'd be lifting his wallet. These girls were fairly brazen, to say the least — even around police officers. I mean, what do you do when one of these girls comes up and asks, "What does it like a tiger and winks?" While she's asking, she looks you in the eyes and winks. Hear that stuff all night and you start forming opinions.

We even get what we call weekend prostitutes — professional men and women with full-time jobs. They come from all over. They've said to themselves, "I can do it, be totally anonymous, lead this secret life, and make a lot of money. Then I'll just stop and go home to my normal life." Most often we arrest them for direct solicitations.

Every police officer enjoys getting pimps off the streets because of the damage they do. One night I stopped two girls in front of the Imperial Palace. They were new girls, and I was pretty sure they were working the street. While I'm dealing with them, this pimp stops his car across the road and starts calling me names. He's shouting out abuse to look big in front of these two girls. By the time I started after him, he'd taken off in his vehicle. A little later, I'm coming down Interstate 15 and I spot the same car. I had a reason to pull him over. These guys aren't exactly the best citizens in the world, and they don't usually keep up-to-date on paying tickets, having driver's licenses and stuff like that. I managed to arrest him and get his car impounded. He ended up hoofing it home in the dark.

But real pleasure came the time I was able to get a pimp to leave town completely. It was about three weeks after I'd bought my house in a development in the northwest part of Las Vegas. I noticed a white and blue Cadillac in the driveway of another house down the street. One night I had someone run its plates. The car came up stolen from a rental company. It's not uncommon among prostitutes to use rental vehicles. Nor is it uncommon for them to forget to pay for them or to return them.

Gradually the picture revealed itself — I was living five doors down from a pimp who was playing house with one of his girls. A successful pimp likes to retain his anonymity and remain kind of out of the scene like this.

It really helped us that the girl had stolen the vehicle. The pimp was now very easily identifiable. We had a clear profile of him. He'd paid for the house with cash, yet he had no visible means of income.

For a week solid after we discovered this guy, he found himself going to jail every night on charges of pandering and living off others. A few days later I stopped his car and was writing him several tickets when I discovered he had recently moved from Phoenix. Turns out he was planning to move his girls from Phoenix to work here. So the guy's giving me his usual lip, complaining that he was always being harassed by us. At the end of it, I said, "Sir, you and I have something in common. We're neighbors." His mouth dropped. Now he realized what we had on him and that we could drag him to jail every night. Shortly after that, his life made miserable by us, he put his house up for sale and moved to Hollywood.

Water Search and Recovery

Special Enforcement Detail, San Diego County, California

"When you're under water scouting for evidence, recovering stolen property, or maybe even hauling in a body, visibility isn't much better than the length of your arm. It's not like weekend diving, with crystal-clear water and spotted fish, that's for sure!"

When you're under water scouting for evidence, recovering stolen property, or maybe even hauling in a body, visibility isn't much better than the length of your arm. It's not like weekend diving, with crystal-clear water and spotted fish, that's for sure! My advice to you is stick to sports diving. It's a lot more fun than what we do.

I got into scuba diving two years ago just so I could be doing this kind of work in our Special Enforcement Detail (SED). Most of us in the tactical response unit are certified divers. Some of us have even attained the rank of master scuba diver or dive master and are pros at underwater search and recovery.

Much of our time is spent training and getting used to diving in zero visibility conditions, when you're more in touch with your environment by probing than actually seeing. Most of the situations I've encountered have been less than thrilling. It's mainly training, and more training always getting prepared for the big one.

Some of the training can be challenging though. Last year, we dove in San Diego Bay in zero conditions. We went below the hull of a large vessel on a silty bottom. Even with diving lights we couldn't see each other and had to feel our way along within a search pattern. You can lose your bearings down there as fast as an octopus slithers under a rock. We had to keep checking just to be sure which way was up and which was down. During the exercise we dropped weapons in the silt and then returned later to search for and retrieve them. It certainly tests your skills, but it also makes you realize what it feels like to be a blind person.

Every second you have to be on guard and keep track of how long you've been down and of your depth. You have to force yourself to breath at a steady pace and not to hyperventilate. And you've got to keep constant track of your partner while incessantly fighting back the urge to panic. Even with trained and experienced divers, it's not unusual to get vertigo.

In one incident last year we got a call to look for a possible body some young kids said

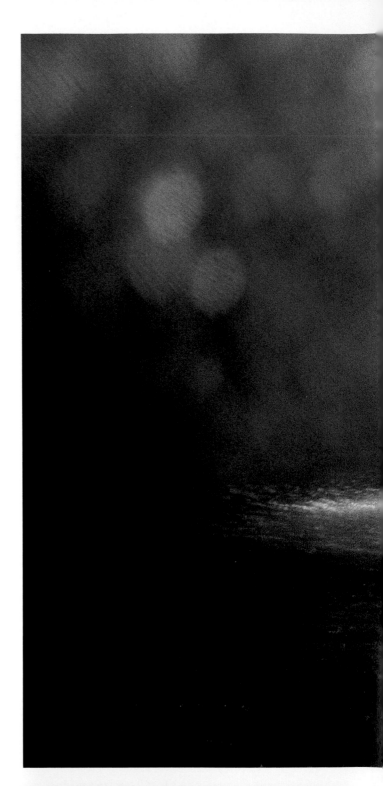

"In the Special Enforcement Detail, we have eighteen deputies, two sergeants, and a lieutenant who work together… If there's a problem, I'm not in a patrol car or on the beat all alone. I'll bring seventeen of my closest friends to an emergency, and we'll take care of it fast!"

was dumped in a neighborhood pond. Most of the time that body'll turn out to be anything but a body, particularly as we heard about this case several days after the children said they saw it. But we went out there, nonetheless, because if you don't check it out, then it'll be a body for sure, and you're caught with egg on your face. When we got there, we found a bait bucket. All we could figure out was that the kids must've stepped on it and the bait or the bucket felt like a human head. That's how they had described it, a human head.

In the Special Enforcement Detail, we have eighteen deputies, two sergeants, and a lieutenant who work together. When we go out on a mission, everyone knows what the other is going to do. It makes us more effective and a lot safer. Working as a team is the best feature of our unit. If there's a problem, I'm not in a patrol car or on the beat all alone. I'll bring seventeen of my closest friends to an emergency, and we'll take care of it *fast*!

I'd say probably half of us have a military background of some kind. I have none. I came into the Sheriff's Department when I was nineteen years old, in the Vietnam era. From my perspective, much of military training isn't applicable to civilian law enforcement. The best combination is a little of both military and civilian experience. Military training is probably best for the discipline. Sometimes the candidate without it doesn't have the fortitude or stick-to-itiveness to endure the physical rigors. The military guys do. Quite a few deputies without prior military experience wash out of the SWAT academy, for instance, because they can't hack it physically.

Previously, I worked in detentions and patrol. Most everyone starts in a jail facility. It's much more routine than SED, and you know when you're gonna get home at night. If it's raining outside, you're dry inside. There's always coffee in the pot, and other cops are always around. Detentions was nice that way, but the bad part was that you're locked up inside all day, which tends to get boring. Did we ever meet the people, though! A regular cross section of them waltzed through there. Everyone from petty thieves to murderers showed up.

The last serious situation our detail had was on Easter. An angry, deranged man shot some rounds off inside his mountain cabin, where he was holed up. When we got called in, we established a perimeter around the house. Eventually he came out and opened fire on us. He wouldn't negotiate, wouldn't put his weapon down, and wouldn't surrender. We returned fire and he was killed. We had no choice.

In one of my earliest call-outs, I was manning a perimeter position outside a house. A sixty-five-pound battering ram — what we call a "doorknocker" — was used to break in the front door. All of a sudden, three shots were fired, and they weren't ours. The bad guy, armed with an AK47, had fired at our men killing one deputy and wounding another. We proceeded to fire chemical agents into his house and peppered it with an MP5 subma- chine gun. We were forced to take this action because we couldn't get the man out to where we could deal with him. The idea was to flush him out. When he finally bolted out the front door, he fired another shot, hitting a deputy sheriff in the finger. That was when we shot him with a barrage of bullets from a shotgun and forty-fives.

One of the deputies who was wounded earlier had been shot in the leg. He then dropped and rolled out of the fatal funnel of the doorway. The other one, who later died, was shot through the upper arm. The bullet broke the arm and severed the aorta so bad that if he'd been shot on an operating table,

they still couldn't have saved him.

The fatal funnel is a very unhealthy place to stand. It's the space in a doorway where you're most vulnerable. Your body is profiled by the light behind, making you a perfect target. Police always stand off to the side when they knock on a door, because many times bad guys will simply respond to a sound at the door with withering gunfire.

I had this overwhelming feeling of helplessness over the killing and wounding of the two officers. There I was, out back, guard- ing against an escape to the rear. I couldn't leave my position to help. I had to carry out my orders. If I'd struck out on my own, the other deputies couldn't depend upon me. That's part of the team concept. You've been assigned a mission, and the mission has to be accomplished. Nonetheless, I wish I could have come to their rescue.

All of us are armed with the Colt .45. It's a venerable standby. Perimeter people carry shotguns as well. They pack a punch, and they're extremely versatile. You can fire a slug, which is one very big and very heavy bullet, or you can just sprinkle buckshot. Chemical agents can also be dispersed with a twelve-gauge.

Cross-training is critical to our team. We have a wide range of skills so we're inter- changeable in any given situation. We all know how to maintain a perimeter or to de- ploy CS gas. The only ones who aren't inter- changeable are the snipers. Snipers are snip- ers. It's a specialty that only a few excel at. However, these marksmen get tapped for other duties as well.

■

We got a report of a teenage girl who was missing. She had been drinking with some kids on some rocks near the spillway at the top of a big dam. We were called in the next day. They lowered the water level of the dam, and our divers went in. I was below the surface going along in next-to-nothing visibility. All of a sudden one of the other men came across a tennis shoe. He thought it was just a tennis shoe that had fallen in. When he grabbed for it, he discovers the body attached to it. He signaled that he'd found something, and we tied a rope to the body and pulled it out. That's basically a lot of what a diver does. But it's such a shock when you find the body. When you see it first hand, it's always darker, a little different than you would expect.

One time we were serving a warrant at a house of one of the local gangs. We believed these guys to be pretty well armed because they'd been feuding with a rival gang and things were escalating. They were expecting a drive-by shooting on their house at any moment. Normally, we'd just go up and knock on the door, but on this one we wanted to lower the risk to ourselves. We surprised them early in the morning and fired flash-bang grenades for a bit of a diversion. It all went very well. Scared the hell out of them. That's what we wanted, the element of surprise. We took control fast, and nobody got hurt. Part of our technique is to create a state of confusion and use it to our advantage. Our business is risk reduction.

The gangs and drive-by shootings are a reality of our business. Gang bullets are killing people in this area on a regular basis. Gang members are not the least bit afraid to shoot. All those bodies stacked in the morgue prove it. We're going up against some serious folk with big guns and sophisticated explosives and countersurveillance measures. Nonetheless, much too often, they're hitting the wrong people. It doesn't matter the color or the ethnic background; they're the wrong people. When the crime's gang- or dope-related and the threat is high, that's usually when they call us in, because it's a problem that the average patrol guy and the average narcotic team are not equipped or trained to confront.

People say we're on the front lines of the narcotics war. Every time you turn around, the cops are finding large caches of narcotics and collaring someone. But, you know, that's just the tip of the iceberg! All this stuff is coming across the border, but the scary part is that it's not like only ten people are using drugs. Sure, we're on the front line, but who are we really protecting? Seems like there's no front line at all. Everybody out front, in the back, and to either side of us is using it!

Homicide

Long Beach, California

"Telling someone that a close relative or friend has been killed is not a pleasant job… It's especially excruciating for me to stop by a house as the bearer of bad news and then, in the midst of the family's inevitable grief and devastation, be forced to leave abruptly to respond to another police call."

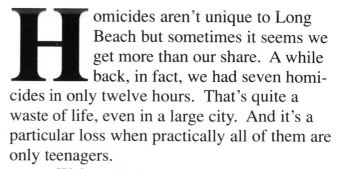

Homicides aren't unique to Long Beach but sometimes it seems we get more than our share. A while back, in fact, we had seven homicides in only twelve hours. That's quite a waste of life, even in a large city. And it's a particular loss when practically all of them are only teenagers.

We've all raised families, owned homes, and mowed the lawn on weekends. We've been through marriages, divorces, love affairs, and everything in between. There isn't a one of us who hasn't lived a full life. But when you see a fourteen- or fifteen-year-old kid die from homicide, you know they've been cheated in the worst way. They've been robbed of life's fine experiences. Here only such a short time, they'll never know how good it can be.

A lot of our homicides are rooted in domestic violence. That's typical throughout the country as well. A fair number also occur as a result of gang activity. These are crimes committed by teenagers who don't appreciate the real value of life. It's a thrill for them to boast they've killed somebody. But in the long run, their adversaries usually retaliate, and they end up victims themselves.

Most of the drug dealers belong to gangs, but these guys are more interested in making money and selling drugs than going out and shooting somebody. Actually, the justification for a gang shooting can be surprisingly insignificant. For example, a member of a rival gang spray-paints his group's logo on the side of a wall in the wrong neighborhood.

The gangs come from all economic and social groups. There are the Longos and the Crips, which are both from deprived areas. Their members live in apartment projects. Then there are the skinheads, who generally come from nice families with good homes and incomes, but, even so, their trademark is violence. It's just a way of life with some of them. They get high on it.

I've seen all kinds of homicides during my time on the force. One man made his six-year-old daughter and four-year-old son drink

drain cleaner. One of the kids died and the other survived, but only after repeated throat surgery. The father drank the stuff, too, and when I got him to the hospital, he was emitting blue fumes from his mouth. He was all broken up about his kids and said he was just trying to get back at his wife after an argument.

One time, another officer and I saw a guy smoking marijuana on the street. We pulled up next to him, and he jumped into a car driven by a female companion. She took off fast, almost pinning me between the two cars. Racing through an intersection, she broadsided a car and killed the occupants, a man and his wife, who was pregnant at the time. Imagine, two people die just because some guy's scared of getting busted for a little grass. You've got to learn to forget these kinds of people, the ones who commit such stupid crimes, or else it will start to haunt you.

These cases are the exception though. Most of our homicides occur because of guns. Everybody's got them. Just a couple of weeks ago, several of our officers stopped a car full of gang members and seized some of the heavy artillery these kids are using these days. They had a twelve-gauge, pump-action shotgun loaded with two types of ammunition — nine pellet shells and pumpkin balls. Pumpkin balls are single slugs so big and heavy they'll blast straight through a car's body, and they certainly won't be stopping for anybody that's sitting in the way. There were also both .22- and .38-caliber revolvers in the vehicle. I doubt these guys were out duck shooting. More likely, they were planning to pull off a drive-by shooting against a rival gang.

To my mind, the best way to eliminate this stuff is to get the guns off the street. There's no reason for people to carry guns around anymore. This isn't the Old West where you need to pack a pistol. We booked one man just last night who had a fully loaded .357 magnum when we stopped his car. The suspect had bought it from a sixteen-year-old gang member only a few minutes earlier. Unfortunately, when this guy goes up before the judge, he'll probably get off easy with a small fine or, at most, four or five days in jail. I

don't think it's right! I saw a bumper sticker a few years ago which said, "Lenient judges make crime pay!" The judge should throw the book at Mr. Macho with his .357 magnum.

When it comes to the officers on the street, we have some pretty good equipment and the choice of any gun we want to carry. If we come up against a situation where we look outgunned, we'll get on the radio and call SWAT, which will arrive with the necessary firepower.

Most of the shooting we see isn't directed at cops. It's gangs firing at gangs. But some is! Just last month, some bad guys on the West Side decided to ambush a police car by getting it to respond to an emergency call. The unit was fired upon by an assault rifle as they arrived at the scene. Some thirty rounds were fired at them, with two penetrating a patrol car. The back of the driver's head was grazed by a bullet, but she was not seriously wounded. The four people who did it were captured and are currently being prosecuted.

These kinds of incidents have a serious impact on us. Each officer that gets fired upon or has a friend injured or killed responds differently, depending on the relationship. Nobody wants to see a comrade shot or killed. It's got to be the saddest duty you'll ever have in this job, attending the funeral of a police buddy who's been taken down.

You never know how an officer is going to respond to the blood and guts he sees on the job. How will he react to seeing, hearing, and smelling death? Once you've smelled it, you never want to smell it again. Some are repulsed. Some have nightmares. Some laugh it off. All are permanently changed at some level.

■

Telling someone that a close relative or friend has been killed in an accident or murdered in the street is not a pleasant job, to say the least. I shudder at the thought of doing it. Nor do I think that a police officer is particularly well trained for the job. Though we're often called on to do it, a minister or someone from the church is probably better equipped to help people through such troubled times. It's especially excruciating for me to stop by a house as the bearer of bad news and then, in the midst of the family's inevitable grief and devastation, be forced to leave abruptly to respond to another police call.

Nothing bothers me so much about being a police officer as to see the young children who die so needlessly. During the Christmas holidays one year, a guy was boasting at a park that he had killed his wife and child. We got wind of it and went to his house to check it out. Looking through the window, I could make out a woman lying on the floor in a pool of blood. She was clearly dead. We forced our way in and found the infant, who had been murdered as well, on the floor in the bedroom. The image of that house lingers with me still — particularly the sight of a fragile, eleven-month-old baby so brutally stabbed.

Another time, actually the first homicide incident I ever saw, a family was traveling at high speed in their small Volkswagen, and a drunk driver crossed over the center divider, colliding head-on with them. The man, his wife, and one small child were killed on impact. Another four-year-old child was crippled for life. It was such an incredible waste!

I guess children are particularly special to me. I worry about who's really watching out for them these days. Take all these youngsters out in the street late at night. You know, responsibility starts at home, so why aren't they there? I really doubt their parents know where they are or what they're doing. The breakdown of the family is a real problem, and society can't simply pass the buck. Parents have to take first responsibility for the welfare of their children.

As a cop, you see your share of violence, and it's curious how each of us adapts to the trauma that comes with the job. I've been shot and stabbed with a knife several times. I was wounded so badly I was out for a month. However, there was no lasting effect — the physical and psychological wounds healed quickly. But even today there are about four spots in this town I simply can't drive by with-

"We've all raised families, owned homes, and mowed the lawn on weekends. We've been through marriages, divorces, love affairs, and everything in between. There isn't a one of us who hasn't lived a full life. But when you see a fourteen-or fifteen-year-old kid die from homicide, you know they've been cheated in the worst way."

out getting emotionally distraught. These are
the places where officers I've known have
been shot. I don't know why, but these are the
incidents that just flash back to me instantly.

For what it's worth, when I was shot, I
was working the plainclothes detail and had
my badge in the breast pocket of my shirt.
The bullet hit the badge and badge holder and
was deflected away from my heart and vital
organs. The badge saved my life — just like
in the movies! But guess what? I don't even
have that badge as a memento. It's still being
held as evidence by the courts.

"As a cop, you see your share of violence… I've been shot and stabbed… the physical and psychological wounds healed quickly. But even today there are about four spots in this town I simply can't drive by without getting emotionally distraught. These are the places where officers I've known have been shot."

Vandalism

Eugene, Oregon

"If lights are getting knocked out, we try to make them taller. We build restrooms more indestructible — like jail cells. We make things vandalproof, but sooner or later they figure out how to destroy them anew. Vandals are pretty ingenious folk."

Joe Cantrell

"Everybody thinks a police officer races around in a patrol car catching crooks and shooting at people. It's not like that. Mostly it's looking for traffic violators and doing reports... We're constantly dealing with an unsavory element of the public, a lot of real bad people and those with morals not quite the same as ours."

It's hard to fathom why three seven-year-old kids would want to burn down a school like they did last week. It's unprecedented in my memory. Such vandalism is nothing less than senseless destruction.

I never fully comprehend any act of vandalism, for that matter. Why does someone purposefully put a scratch down the side of a nice new car with a key? Is it envy? Why do people deface and damage public phones and bathrooms? Is it because they've had a drink and thrown their inhibitions out the window? Most vandalism seems to be drink-related, in fact. Alcohol definitely seems to reduce people's respect for public property. They do things they would never do sober, but have secretly probably wanted to do for years.

We had one guy cut loose in a football stadium with a .233 automatic rifle shooting the hell out of scoreboards, huge glass VIP windows, just about everything. Finally he shot a runner and then turned the gun on himself. Did this begin as vandalism and then the guy got totally carried away? Sure, there were traces of drugs in his system, but we're talking vandalism turned homicide. He didn't leave any clues, so we'll never know why.

We don't get much vandalism inside the city proper. Most of what we experience occurs in the night at the city limits. However, we did have a case not that long ago when the windows of cars and shops were being shot out with some frequency. We got a tip on the license plate of the car that was doing it. We just went to his place of residence and waited him out. He showed up eventually, and he had the pellet gun he had been using with him. We booked him on a few more charges than simply breaking windows. And we haven't had another outbreak of such vandalism since.

The most common kind of vandalism is graffiti, closely followed by destruction of public property. Vandalism costs the taxpayer literally millions of dollars each year. And it results in a reduction of public facilities and services. A good example of this is at a park on the city limits. It's a pretty area, frequented by courting couples. The pay phones have

Joe Cantrell

been destroyed so often that the phone company has given up repairing them. If someone is in trouble and needs a phone, they won't find one there now. The bathrooms get damaged so often that they are seldom operational. And occasionally punks tear up the grass with their vehicles and smash out the overhead lights with stones.

We're always searching for new ways to combat vandalism. If lights are getting knocked out, we try to make them taller. We build restrooms more indestructible — like jail cells. We make things vandalproof, but sooner or later they figure out how to destroy them anew. Vandals are pretty ingenious folk.

We've tried to make the punishment fit the crime. Fines don't work with everyone, so we've introduced community work programs for most vandalism crimes. This seems to be a very effective method of punishing offenders.

■

I haven't actually caught anybody spray-painting the walls, but, doggone it, I can't wait until the moment I do. The city owns these bridges, and these people are just defacing them, ruining them with graffiti. It's blatant disrespect for authority. Usually all we find is just the empty paint cans. It takes a lot of luck to catch them in the act.

Over behind the shopping center, there's a lot of the gang-type graffiti, the Crips and the Bloods. I don't know if it's real, but more and more of it is showing up. I think a lot of it is by wannabees. It's their method of communication and of trying to be tough.

"Most vandalism seems to be drink-related. Alcohol definitely seems to reduce people's respect for public property. They do things they would never do sober, but have secretly probably wanted to do for years."

Unfortunately, most of the graffiti we're finding is profanity — just some guy writing dirty words on the wall. They say graffiti's not a big crime. It's just defacing a wall with a drawing of God or whatever image. But writing filthy words — that's just outrageous! It's like a person going out in public and flipping the bird at someone, you know, the middle finger. Or a person talking like a sewer in front of kids. There's no law against it. They've pumped up the Constitution to make it a protected thing. You can say and write whatever you like, no matter how filthy or prejudiced it may be. And what really bugs me is they can do it right in front of women and children. You're not supposed to be doing that kind of stuff in front of them.

Everybody thinks a police officer races around in a patrol car catching crooks and shooting at people. It's not like that. Mostly it's looking for traffic violators and doing reports. We do see a lot of things other people don't see. We're constantly dealing with an unsavory element of the public, a lot of real bad people and those with morals not quite the same as ours. But paperwork is a big part of the job, and you've got to be competent at it.

■

I've been on the force for a long time now, and one thing that stays the same is the vandalism. People just go out and damage property for who knows what reason. They break car antennas and windows, they dump piles of garbage in public places. It just continues to occur, year after year, regardless of the changes in society. What's new in the last few years is the gang graffiti. Gangs are nothing new to New York, but we haven't had them so much before on the West Coast, except for Los Angeles maybe. The racial graffiti is more noticeable, too.

A lot of the gang graffiti is not actually done by members, but it creates the perception in the community that a gang problem exists. It's a two-edged sword. On the one side, it alerts people to deal with the problem before the gangs get out of hand. On the other side,

a lot of the stuff that emblazons walls causes negative racial feelings against blacks, who are the most prominent members in West Coast street gangs. The white supremacists aggravate these feelings as well with all their racist slogans.

The Eugene police force tries its best to get this stuff off the walls as fast as possible. Usually it's gone within forty-eight hours. It's worth the expense because it eliminates the impression in the community that gangs are pervasive.

When we see graffiti that's gang-related, racist, or both, it's brought to the attention of our investigators. They've photographed most of the graffiti that's shown up, and they know how to spot themes that should concern us. They've studied graffiti from Los Angeles to Portland, so they can make heads or tails of what's legitimate gang graffiti or simply some guy trying to imitate it. For example, we found what we thought was gang graffiti, but then realized it was written in the wrong color. It was sprayed in red, but if it'd been legit, it would have been in blue, the color of that particular gang. Never red! Never ever red! By doing our homework, we were able to ferret that one out.

The legitimate gang graffiti is pretty informative. It's not like an underground newspaper where we would have to infiltrate the group just to get a copy. But you have to be somewhat skeptical of the tough tone. There is an element of bravado that may not reflect the truth.

Our ability to respond to vandalism and graffiti is limited. Our budget's not fat, we have to prioritize everything. The population of Eugene has risen, and the number of police calls right along with it. Serious crimes have increased as well. We have a much greater workload than five years ago, but we have the same level of resources. Unfortunately, because graffiti is a property crime and not of direct harm to people, it's way down the scale in terms of priority.

K9 Unit

King County, Seattle, Washington

"Zach saved my life and those with me. I can't pay a bigger tribute to him than saying that. These dogs are all loyal to us, and every one of them would have done the same thing. It's a great loss, as great as losing any partner."

"On the job I'm seldom apprehensive. That may sound strange, but my dog, Luke, is well trained to do his job. I love him dearly, and I don't want to lose him, but the risk is there every day. But then Luke risks losing me every day, too."

Whenever it's dangerous for an officer to search or the physical access is limited, we get a dog on it. The K9 unit does certain tasks safely and effectively, particularly checking large areas, such as warehouses, and small, tight ones, like under buildings and in crawl spaces or attics.

People are the biggest obstacle for our dogs. If there are too many of them in the search area, the scent of the crook gets contaminated. The dog will pick up the smell of other people, including the police officers. It's because each person has his own particular scent. But our dogs are taught to discriminate one scent from another. If an area has been contaminated with other scents, it makes tracking harder, but not impossible.

While these dogs have been trained for a variety of tasks, we don't generally use them for search and rescue. Maybe in an emergency, when an accident victim has wandered off or something, we'll use them, but their principal job is to track violators.

Last year I lost my dog to just such a violator. It was a year ago, the sixth of July, seven o'clock in the evening. We had a car chase down in a little community about ten miles south of Seattle. Our patrol unit was chasing a BMW stolen from Utah. The guy was wanted there for homicide. He was wanted in California for 10 armed robberies. And we wanted him here for check fraud and a whole bunch of other things.

He pulled into a lot and took off on foot, over a fence and into the woods. I arrived shortly after that with my dog, Zach. We tracked this man for two hundred yards, and then Zach found him in the brush, close by the freeway. He had a gun and was ready to take down whoever approached him. He shot Zach four times in the head and then apparently shot himself. After we waited a while, another K9 unit was called in and found the two dead.

We're not absolutely sure if the suspect shot himself intentionally. We think it may have been an accident, given the evidence and where the wound was in the head. But we just don't know for sure. We hope it was an accident. The dog may have continued to struggle after he was shot and forced the weapon back against the suspect.

Zach saved my life and those with me. I can't pay a bigger tribute to him than saying that. These dogs are all loyal to us, and every one of them would have done the same thing. It's a great loss, as great as losing any partner.

We'd never had a dog killed in the line of duty before, and ironically, Zach's father, Jake, had also been shot. He was shot three times, once in the head following a bank robbery. Jake survived it and now lives in retirement. It's unique that both father and son should be shot like that.

■

I chose the K9 unit because I love dogs and have had them all my life. Joining the unit gave me an opportunity every police officer wants — to catch those criminals who've gotten away and who don't normally get caught. K9 officers are out in front every time, and we usually get our man, far more often than the officer who has no dog.

Being a K9 handler involves more of your life than normal policework. The dog's a part of the family and a constant reminder that you're subject to call twenty-four hours a day.

On the job I'm seldom apprehensive. That may sound strange, but my dog, Luke, is well trained to do his job. I love him dearly, and I don't want to lose him, but the risk is there every day. But then Luke risks losing me every day, too. If we do things right, it won't happen, but you can't get it right every time, so certainly the possibility is there. If I thought the possibility was that great, I wouldn't be in the unit. I couldn't work the dog if I was constantly afraid of losing him. Anyway, he would pick up on it right away, and it would diminish his effectiveness.

When I'm exhilarated, the dog's spirits soar as well. We both do a better job together then, so that's the level you always try to maintain. If I'm down in the dumps, which can happen, the dog ends up joining me down there, and we both can get bad names.

Peter Hendrie

"Luke was donated to the department, and I did all the training along with an experienced dog trainer. Actually, it was more a case of dog and handler being trained together. We were two greenhorns, and I learned as Luke learned. Now we're a team…"

I've seen him startled, but I've never seen him scared. Dogs don't seem to have the same fears as humans. But, boy, if they're shocked or startled, they'll react almost immediately, not get immobilized with fear. It's amazing how they can respond so fast.

A police officer is nothing more than a social worker who deals with problems other people can't handle. Luke and I often get the worst problems. Sometimes it's chasing down a person who just doesn't want to be caught. They're running hard, and we've no idea whether they're armed or not. Nor do we know whether they're mentally in control. That's when I really need a dog, or else I'd be in a spot. I lost my weapon during one fight. It was on the ground between me and the assailant. The dog took the subject to the ground, and I was able to recover and holster my weapon.

At such times, you haven't got time to be afraid; your mind is working on how to cope. Afterwards, you wonder what might have happened to you and your dog. Then you break into a cold sweat and do all sorts of things. But, you know, I've been doing this for a little over sixteen years. The reactions are instinctive, and I don't think of the ramifications of these situations until later.

Dogs can be incredibly patient as well. For example, waiting out a situation, sometimes for as much as four or five hours, you can put these dogs into a down state where they're on the ground and relaxing fairly comfortably. But if you have an extremely hyper dog, then you've got problems.

Luke was donated to the department, and I did all the training along with an experienced dog trainer. Actually, it was more a case of dog and handler being trained together. We were two greenhorns, and I learned as Luke learned. Now we're a team, and nobody else handles him.

Luke is also an absolutely perfect house pet, playing and fetching for the kids. The whole family loves him. But he's been trained to be aggressive and to react positively in surroundings like heavy brush and gunfire. The dog's best protection from injury is to attack the source. If someone reaches out with a gun and starts firing, then the dog leaps in from the side and takes that gun. Unfortunately, it doesn't always work that way, but that's the idea. If Luke were passive, then he'd be nothing but a target. Then we'd both be in trouble.

Driving Under the Influence

Anchorage, Alaska

"Alcohol consumption is the most deadly recreation in this state. Ninety percent of the problems I get on the highway in these early hours are alcohol-related. Somebody's always drunk. If it's not the driver, then it's the passengers. And it's the period when shootings usually occur. Drinking — that's what triggers most of them!"

Alcohol consumption is the most deadly recreation in this state. Ninety percent of the problems I get on the highway in these early hours are alcohol-related. Somebody's always drunk. If it's not the driver, then it's the passengers. And it's the period when shootings usually occur. Drinking — that's what triggers most of them!

Alaska, because it's so far north, has real long summer days. Most people are busy doing seasonal work or are on commercial fishing boats. Since the oil spill, a lot of people have jobs doing cleanup. It's not that less drinking is occurring than normal, it's just that most of these people are not in town. In the wintertime, there's all that darkness and the long nights. Drunk driving is a problem because people don't have much to do. If you don't snow-ski or use snow machines, or like being out in the cold, you end up drinking. That's when the serious accidents occur.

Early this morning I noticed this guy turn onto the highway. From a distance, I thought I saw him run a red light. Once he'd made the turn, he drove on the far edge of the road and then came back onto the highway. I was pretty sure he was drunk. The car crossed the center line a few more times, almost into the next lane. We pulled him over, and I could smell alcohol on him and see the drunken signs, the slurred speech, bloodshot eyes, and unsteady balance. He didn't want to take a sobriety test because he figured that if he didn't take it, I couldn't arrest him. So I promptly arrested him anyway. He was real upset. On the drive to the station, I made him give a sample of his breath for the faxsimiter. He kept yelling, "You're wasting your time. You'll never prove I was drunk." He was yelling for us to get him his lawyer. Of course, he refused the Breathalyzer. I read him the fine print, the consent warning that basically says if a person is arrested for driving while intoxicated, he is then required to give a breath sample. If he refuses, then it's another arrestable offense and the penalties are the same as for driving intoxicated.

This guy made me a little more appre-

"Drunk driving is a problem because people don't have much to do. If you don't snow-ski or use snow machines, or like being out in the cold, you end up drinking. That's when the serious accidents occur."

hensive than normal. He was so abusive! But I'm six-feet-four inches and weigh 242 pounds. I don't usually have problems with drunks, particularly when other police are involved. If it had been just me alone, it'd be different. My bigger concern usually is that if some kind of physical altercation actually takes place, and I hurt somebody, they immediately start hollering "police brutality."

■

Alcohol abuse is a real serious problem in Alaska. The drunks come from every social stratum. It's not an ethnic thing. All kinds do it, and it takes its toll on society. Our police force spends an extraordinary amount of time dealing with drunk drivers. When we arrest someone for driving under the influence, or DUI as we call it, it takes two hours of an officer's time just to process the guy. Then there's all the paperwork, the court costs, and the rehabilitation.

All of us on the force get discouraged by the amount of time we spend dealing with it. And even then we can end up losing because of the legal system. There was a case where a sharp defense attorney came along and quizzed an officer in court on his in-depth knowledge of chemical reactions. A normal officer probably has about two years chemistry in high school, and that was about twenty years ago. That's hardly enough to grasp the subtle reactions of alcohol in the blood and its effect on body metabolism. The lawyer ended up making him look fairly ignorant, if not foolish, in front of the jury. And his client took a walk!

DUI refers to both alcohol and drugs. With alcohol, we consider a driver intoxicated if he has a reading of .10. If it's in the .05 to .10 range, he's considered impaired. The cop then has to demonstrate in court that the person was impaired to the point of being unable to drive. Often, in these cases, the driver is messed up, but it's because of other drugs like marijuana or prescription pills. If the driver's reading is below .05, we toss him back.

About five years ago, we had a special unit to fight drunk driving. It was called the Drunkbusters and was most active during the holidays — Thanksgiving to New Year's — when the most drunks were pouring themselves into cars. Unfortunately, budget cuts have busted the Drunkbusters. Normal police units now go after DUIs as a part of their overall duties.

Driver education is one of the best ways to curb drunk driving. Right when kids first get their licenses, the dangers and the risks of driving intoxicated should be hammered into their heads. Go into the schools and talk to them about what insanity it is. Let them know that it doesn't just happen to the other guy.

Some excellent advertisements against drunk driving have been created. Kids seem to really respond to them. I have an eight-year-old who thinks they're terrific. One TV ad says, "Driving while drunk can kill a friendship." It shows a car crash and dead teenagers and ends with a skeleton's hand. This is pretty graphic stuff in a child's mind. These advertisements hopefully will give us a generation who won't want to drink and drive.

One major thing we've done to curb DUI is to strengthen our state laws against those repeat offenders. In a couple of cases where injury or death has occurred because of a drunk, the intoxicated driver got convicted with assault and even murder. More and more drivers now know we mean business.

It's a battle, but I think we're winning it. Not just because of the strict penalties, but because of peer pressure from the community itself. Everybody is participating! If you host a party now, you're probably going to watch your guests, check whether they're getting all boozed up or not. Twenty years ago, people would dance on tables with lamp shades on their heads. Now they feel inhibited to become really drunk, even at a private party.

Fear of lawsuits has had an influence as well. A lot of liquor stores and bars won't let you get tanked up for fear you'll drive down the road and run over somebody. Then the next of kin will sue the establishment that supplied the booze. The community has been behind us 100 percent in holding proprietors more responsible. Mothers Against Drunk Driving (MADD) and other groups in Anchorage, such as CHAR-ARBA (Cabaret Hotel and Restaurant Association-Anchorage Restaurant and Beverage Association), have raised the consciousness of everyone. Bartenders now keep an eye out for people leaving their premises bombed and make them ride home with a sober friend or take a cab. Some cab companies now offer someone who's had a few too many a reduced rate or a free trip home. We're now seeing a significant reduction in alcohol-related traffic deaths.

Hopefully, some of this new technology you hear about is going to further decrease the number of DUI incidents in the future. Controlled ignitions with Breathalyzers, complicated car locks — these things hold real promise. Unfortunately, not many of them are yet practical, and it will probably be a long time before a lot of people have access to them.

The typical response of a drunk is, "Why are you bothering me? Why aren't you out there catching real criminals?" That's always the line. One or two have actually said, "I'm sorry. Thank you for arresting me. I probably would have hurt somebody." But, boy, that's the exception! The intoxicated person just doesn't see it as a crime. In his mind, he's thinking, "I'm perfectly capable of handling it. I'm not going to hurt anyone." The idea of going to jail is just beyond their comprehension. Only bad people go to jail, and they certainly don't perceive themselves as being criminals.

Specialized Services

Honolulu, Hawaii

"The incident will usually be hot. Nine times out of ten, it's about to explode and is life-threatening to civilians in the vicinity and the officers who arrive. This is when we get the call. We're like SWAT… a heavy-duty response to society's most hostile crimes —a necessary evil if you know what I mean."

The incident will usually be hot. Nine times out of ten, it's about to explode and is life-threatening to civilians in the vicinity and the officers who arrive. This is when we get the call. We're like the SWAT units that employ special weapons and tactics in police departments nationwide. Honolulu Police Department's Specialized Services Division (SSD) is a heavy-duty response to society's most hostile crimes — a necessary evil, if you know what I mean.

Before anyone can join SSD, or most SWAT units for that matter, they go through a tough selection process. He or she needs to be physically fit just to be considered. If a police officer can run a mile under eight minutes, do seventy sit-ups and a ten-kilometer run, then that person has got a chance. Next we check with the officer's supervisor to see what kind of cop he or she really is. We only want those who can stand up to stress.

Officers assigned to SSD have to maintain a firm grip on their emotions. You just can't get emotionally involved in the situations we confront. You've got to respond to the crisis with the training you've received and at all times remain unemotional.

In Honolulu, SSD's public image shines. It's because we never respond to a problem violently. If we went out and killed the suspect every time, our image would be far different than it is today. The SWAT philosophy is first "negotiate" to neutralize any problem. Ninety-nine-point-nine percent of the time, we're successful at it. We intervene with terrorists, criminals, and the crazies — always trying to avoid bloodshed. Our record is a better measure of our effectiveness than dollars and cents, and it certainly shows we're responding to a public need to curb violence.

Being a member of SSD is a full-time job. I carry a beeper at all times. I'm on call at all hours. When the beeper goes off and an incident is taking place, it's adrenaline city! You have to control that adrenaline rush, particularly during endless hours of waiting at the scene. Nothing's happening. You can hear the negotiations drone on and on. But at any mo-

"When the beeper goes off... it's adrenaline city! You have to control that adrenaline rush, particularly during endless hours of waiting at the scene. Nothing's happening. You can hear the negotiations drone on and on. But at any moment, you might get the order to go, and things immediately change 180 degrees."

ment, you might get the order to go, and things immediately change 180 degrees. Last night we had a typical SSD call-out. An argument escalated to violence. A man ran into his house and barricaded himself inside. When we got the word that it was a hostile situation, the adrenaline pumped. The fears just raced through our minds. What are we going to encounter? How are they armed? Fortunately, the guy last night gave himself up. It was just another day for us.

■

Even the smallest incidents can quickly get out of hand, so we tend to proceed extremely cautiously. Things seldom happen as fast as you see them on TV. Sometimes, however, all the negotiating in the world won't get you anywhere. It happened once when I was sergeant. An estranged husband, armed with a small caliber handgun was holding his wife and kid hostage. While we were removing officers from the inner perimeter, the hostages managed to escape.

We tried to reason with the man by phone and bullhorn, but he just wouldn't respond, no matter what we said or how loud we said it. His wife gave us a detailed plan of the house, so we decided to go in. We did a room-by-room search until we hit the bedroom where he was supposed to be.

There he was, lying on a bed, gun in hand. He was fast asleep! Several of us held him down while we grabbed the gun from his hand. Not surprisingly, I learned later that the offender had been drinking heavily.

In the eleven years I've been with this unit, I can only think of four instances in which we had to go in. All the others have been handled successfully through skillful negotiations. Only once, in my recollection, has there been a loss of human life in a hostage, barricade, or sniper incident.

Two guys had escaped from a local jail, and one of them, who had an AK47, took a family with small children hostage in their apartment. The escapee demanded that a friend of his be summoned there. The friend consented, thinking he would convince the gunman to surrender. In exchange for the friend, we managed to persuade the gunman to let the family go.

Two officers also went in to negotiate further. One officer was released soon after, supposedly to follow up on the escapee's demands. The other was let go a little later. This all took place over approximately a fourteen-hour period. By this time, negotiations began to get quite hostile, and the gunman started firing indiscriminate bursts from the windows.

We decided to vacate the building, though many people were reluctant to go. As the range of fire was over the front door of the building, we had to break out the shutters on back windows and evacuate people in that direction. That left the gunman inside alone with his reluctant friend. Negotiations had collapsed and the man was cutting loose sporadically with his AK47. That's when we decided to use teargas.

We waited until the fire apparatus and other emergency personnel were in place and then fired in the pyrotechnic-discharged teargas. The apartment immediately started to catch fire, and the gunman's buddy saved himself by jumping through the window. The gunman barricaded himself in the bathroom. Even with the building in flames, the firemen were naturally reluctant to proceed. After about twenty or thirty minutes, a SSD team entered the place and found the escapee dead, asphyxiated by the heat and fumes.

As with all homicides, an investigation followed. The prosecuting attorney's office labeled it "justifiable homicide," which it obviously was. Looking back, it's sad, but inevitable — the only real loss in all my years of responding to violent confrontation. We can't win them all, but our record speaks for itself.

Legends and Heroes

In this chapter, we pay homage to the best in American policework by honoring the qualities of courage, sacrifice and commitment — the very lifeblood of those who are truly legends and heroes. Nominations for the officers we single out were received from police departments nationwide. By honoring these few, we also honor the many other officers, living and dead, who deserve similar recognition.

What do we mean by legend? The definition of a legend is a "notable person whose deeds or exploits are talked about in his time." Obviously the number of American police officers that fit this definition is sizable, making it unavoidable that some very deserving nominees be excluded. One example of this is Officer Barry Miller, whose record includes more DUI arrests than all his co-workers combined; the most felony arrests; and the most drug busts. He recently "adopted" and cleaned up a drug-infested housing project that was so bad his commanding officer said, "Most officers label this a punishment assignment... Why Miller asked for it still mystifies me." Or Senior Patrol Officer Jim Wolsch, known as "Stoop-Down" by people in the street, who with his dog, Jack the Ripper, seized $6,849,848 worth of drugs, $365,514 in currency and eight vehicles, and made over 178 arrests.

Official records about exceptional officers omitted the nuances of first-hand knowledge. Take Sergeant Thomas Quirk, an ex-paratrooper, a recipient of the Purple Heart and other medals for valor. Testimony from one of his men declared, "He loves being a cop. When something's going on, he's right there, always thinking about his men, not about himself — the guy's unreal!" There are others who deserve recognition in this chapter as well. They include Major Charles Bennett, Officer Tom Betts, Corporal David McCamley, and Sergeant Joe Sede, to name but a few.

While most of the officers profiled here are still living, two are not. They represent a small fraction of the more than 150 U.S. officers killed in the line of duty annually. We received nominations for many officers killed in the line of duty, including Corporal Charles Hill and Officers Thomas Gill and Sherman Griffith. While we are honoring officers who are currently serving or fairly recently retired, it was difficult to overlook such candidates as Captain Edgar Crosswell, the officer whose initiative resulted in the identification of major Mafia figures; Detective John Shannahan, whose records on the Fulton Market and the Genovese family are so extensive they have recently been computerized and are being used in several ongoing investigations; and Officer Frank Feldhaus, affectionately labeled "Pappy" by residents of the beat he policed from 1937 to 1977.

And what is a hero? A hero is a person "admired for courage or nobility of exploit." While we received numerous nominations, we can only include a few. Among the deserving nominees we were unable to put in the book are several who risked their lives to rescue people in fires — Officers Steve Godrey, Allen Lowy and Albert Taylor. And then there's David Benoit, who managed to save sixty people in two separate incidents.

Many officers who are not featured here have demonstrated heroic qualities as well. Consider Sergeants Donald Flusche and William Temple, who both overcame odds of three to one to foil armed assaults in separate incidents. Their exploits did not stop there. Sergeant Flusche went on to establish an alcohol-abuse program and Sergeant Temple set up a post-shooting trauma course for his fellow officers.

Other officers meriting recognition include Officer Richard Bert, who, when seriously wounded in a crack bust, fought off his assailants, collapsed in the arms of his fellow officers, and, realizing their distress at his serious, but nonfatal, injuries, kept assuring them he was okay and not to worry; Officer Susan La Gray who scared off a knife-wielding rapist while off duty; Sergeant Kenneth Pollock, who averted a major highway pileup and saved a family from personal harm by selflessly driving his car between theirs and another which was headed straight at them out of control; and Officer Tim Ryan, who saved a brother and sister from drowning when the girl was trying to commit suicide.

Some nominations consisted of exceptional teams of officers. It was a difficult selection, with some great teams narrowly missing out, including the one that curbed the FALN (responsible for over a hundred bombings in Puerto Rico and on the U.S. mainland), and the team of Lieutenant Lyle Edwards and Detective Mike McClary, who followed a drug trail from Los Angeles to Chiang Mai, Thailand.

Officers have been chosen for Legends and Heroes on the basis of their success in creating innovative community programs or new policing methods and for their deeds of heroism and general career excellence.

In one case, we have selected an outstanding candidate who wasn't even a police officer — a police dog named Zach. Zach gave his life proving that canines are not only man's best friend but, sometimes, an officer's very best partner as well.

All the officers in this chapter exemplify the very best attributes of police life, the stuff of legends and heroes. We salute them and the many others who, sharing their attributes, stand without question in the ranks of America's finest.

Legends and Heroes

Detectives Alex Alvarez, Jose Diaz, Jorge Plasencia
Metro-Dade Police Department
Miami, Florida

In July 1985 three male bodies were found floating in the Miami River. A routine investigation of what seemed to be routine homicides among drug dealers soon widened into a case that resulted in charges being brought against Miami police officers as drug-dealing co-conspirators. The Miami River Cops Case became one of the most significant police corruption cases in the history of Dade County. Detectives Alex Alvarez, Jorge Plasencia and Jose Diaz spearheaded the investigation. All three officers were experienced investigators with the Homicide Bureau's elite CENTAC 26 Squad, which targets organized drug-related violence. In preparation for a complex trial that lasted several months, the three bilingual detectives managed to enlist the cooperation of more than 124 U.S. and foreign witnesses, several of them drug traffickers who had been victims themselves. The tireless investigative efforts of Alvarez, Diaz, and Plasencia led to the arrest of eight class-one drug traffickers and the seizure of 384 kilograms of cocaine, $1.5 million in U.S. currency, $200,000 in real property, nine automobiles, and three vessels. The three detectives received the Exceptional Service Award and shared Distinguished Officer of the Month honors for August 1987.

A native of Havana, Cuba, Jose Diaz joined the Metro-Dade Police Department in 1975, and has been both a uniformed officer and a detective. Jorge Plasencia, also from Havana, has been with Metro-Dade since 1976, and has served in uniformed patrol, general investigations, and Vice-Intelligence-Narcotics before being assigned to Homicide. Alex Alvarez joined Metro-Dade in 1980, and is currently with the Tactical Section of the Special Investigations Division.

Officer Greg Armstrong
Tallahassee Police Department
Tallahassee, Florida

On July 8, 1988, Officer Greg Armstrong and his partner, Officer Ernie Ponce de Leon, were dispatched to investigate four suspicious persons in a car parked behind a laundromat. It turned out that three of the suspects were armed and desperate fugitives from a Maryland prison. Within moments, what began as a routine call erupted into a violent shoot-out that left Officer Ponce de Leon dead from gunshot wounds to the chest and Officer Armstrong with no support. He found cover and, while returning the gunfire, managed to send out detailed calls for backup and an ambulance. All three suspects were seriously wounded and eventually taken into custody, charged with murder and attempted murder. Officer Armstrong managed to escape injury. His reactions in the face of overwhelming odds provide an extraordinary example of clear thinking and textbook composure. While heroic by any standards, his achievement becomes all the more astonishing when his age and level of experience are taken into account. At the time of the shooting, Officer Armstrong was a twenty-three-year-old rookie officer who had completed his basic training just two months earlier.

Since then, Officer Armstrong has won an impressive roster of awards: he received the Tallahassee Police Department's highest tribute, the Medal of Valor, and was named Law Enforcement Officer of the Year for Florida's Big Bend by a group of local business and civic leaders. On July 20, 1988, Florida Governor Bob Martinez proclaimed that day Officer Greg Armstrong Day. Such accolades have not fazed Armstrong, who, much to his credit, prefers to remain outside the limelight in order to continue the normal duties of a young police officer and to gain experience in his profession. Prior to his career with the Tallahassee Police Department, Officer Armstrong spent two years in the United States Army, where he was a paratrooper in the 82nd Airborne Division.

Officer Wilfred Barriere
Port Authority of New York and New Jersey
Police Department
Queens, New York

On November 24, 1986, at 4:15 A.M., Officer Wilfred Barriere of the Port Authority of New York and New Jersey Police Department stopped for coffee at the Sage Diner with his two partners. While everything appeared calm as they approached, two armed men had just pistol-whipped an employee and robbed the patrons inside the diner. Officer Barriere's suspicions were first aroused when he noticed a vehicle with no license plates parked at the side of the diner. As the officer approached the car, shots rang out. His partners, who had just entered the diner, were wounded and now lay exposed to further fire. Acting quickly and with little regard for his own safety, Barriere managed to draw the attention of one of the gunmen and shot him several times during an exchange of gunfire (the other suspect escaped through the back of the diner, but was later caught when he sought treatment for a chest wound). Officer Barriere then managed to guard the prisoner and protect the scene while ensuring that his partners both received prompt medical treatment. Had it not been for Officer Barriere's quick thinking and courage in drawing fire, his partners might not have survived the incident.

During the course of his distinguished eighteen-year career, Officer Barriere has received the Port Authority Medal of Honor, the New York Governor's Police Officer of the Year Award, the Nassau County Police Shield's Officer of the Month Award, three Meritorious Police Duty Medals, and nine Excellent Police Duty Medals. He is married and the father of three young children.

Officer Wayne Darrell Barton
Boca Raton Police Department
Boca Raton, Florida

Officer Wayne Darrell Barton personifies idealism, dedication, and hard work in service to others. Since his first day with the Boca Raton Police Department, he has been a tireless worker on behalf of underprivileged children and a leader in the struggle against narcotics in the community. Having been raised in a poor, high-crime neighborhood, Officer Barton knows the impact such an environment has on kids — both his younger and older brothers are now in prison. While not entirely eliminating the scourge of drugs, his diligence in applying pressure against dealers has clearly paid off in a noticeable drop in street-level activity within his beat. Providing educational opportunities also has been a priority for Officer Barton. With his assistance, the housing authority set up an after-school program dedicated to teaching problem children from the Pearl City community, a poor and drug-ridden section of Boca Raton. He is also responsible for a community cleanup program there and has devoted many summers to the recreation programs set up for children by the Deerfield Beach Recreation Department.

Officer Barton has been repeatedly commended by various civic groups. He was named Officer of the Year by the Boca Raton Police Department in 1987, and was profiled in *Parade* magazine in 1988. He was one of nine officers around the country who received awards from the International Association of Chiefs of Police and *Parade*.

Officer Rick Bass
Escondido Police Department
Escondido, California

The first week of December 1987 was a big one for Officer Rick Bass of the Escondido Police Department. The city of Escondido was hit by two catastrophes that week. In the first, the Hyundai auto dealership was devastated by a $1.5 million arson fire that nearly destroyed the entire inventory of new cars, those being serviced and all of the company's business records. In the second, a man opened fire with an assault weapon in his apartment complex, endangering those in the vicinity. By the time he was killed, nineteen hours later, the gunman had killed a sheriff's SWAT team member and wounded two others. Detective Rick Bass led the investigations of both these incidents, overseeing evidence gathering and scene processing. In the arson fire Detective Bass uncovered important physical evidence left behind by the suspect that directly linked the suspect to the fire. The case was the largest successful conviction of arson in San Diego County history. In the sniper incident Detective Bass led a highly complicated investigation and even examined a controversy about the officers' conduct. With the evidence Officer Bass gathered, he was able to clear law enforcement officials of any improper conduct.

A thirteen-year veteran of law enforcement, Detective Bass has received numerous Commanding Officer Citations for his exceptional evidence-collecting and -processing capabilities, as well as for his interrogative techniques. His commitment to service has been an example to many young men and women who enter law enforcement through the department's Explorer Program.

Officer Charles Beasley (deceased)
Detroit Police Department
Detroit, Michigan

On November 22, 1988, Officer Charles Beasley was working in an undercover assignment, posing as a midlevel narcotics dealer involved in a deal to purchase a kilo of cocaine in exchange for $25,000. Without warning, one of the subjects pulled a gun and fatally shot the thirty-nine-year-old officer, tragically ending his distinguished career in the Detroit Police Department's 7th Precinct. From his very first night of duty in the patrol car, when he fatally wounded two gunmen who had shot his partner, Officer Beasley could always be counted upon to act courageously and selflessly in carrying out his duties. Aside from earning the respect and admiration of his partners and superiors, he was the recipient of numerous awards and letters of commendation from the department, including a citation in 1986 for the extraordinary rescue of a young child when no emergency medical vehicles were available.

Officer Fred Casale
Clearwater Police Department
Clearwater, Florida

On June 16, 1982, an inmate escaped from the Pinellas County Jail and a BOLO (Be on the look out) was broadcast to neighboring law enforcement communities. The fugitive eluded capture by heading for the sparsely populated coast rather than the urban areas, where he would more easily blend in with the general population. Using his knowledge of the coastal areas and its many opportunities for concealment, Officer Fred Casale began an extensive search beneath docks, piers, and other man-made structures, leading to the subject's eventual recapture. He was also instrumental in numerous felony arrests on Clearwater Beach when open abuse of narcotics became a problem. And it was thanks to Officer Casale's actions that a man displaying dangerous firearms on Big Pier 60 was captured without harm to any of the numerous tourists in the area.

A native of Brooklyn, New York, Officer Casale is best known in Clearwater as "Officer Friendly," who visits preschool and elementary school classes and delivers highly popular lectures on safety and crime awareness. His concern for the welfare of the community, especially young people, has earned him numerous awards, including the Clearwater Jaycees Outstanding Police Officer of the Year Award in 1981, the Florida House of Representatives' Outstanding Law Enforcement Officer of the Year in 1982, and recognition from the United States Senate in 1985 for Outstanding Volunteer Service.

Officer Joseph Emanuel Davis (deceased)
Atlanta Police Department
Atlanta, Georgia

In the early morning hours of June 7, 1989, Officer Joseph Emanuel Davis captured a robbery suspect and put him in the back of his patrol car. He then went in pursuit of a second suspect. In the course of this chase Officer Davis was shot dead with his own service revolver. Officer Davis's seven-year career was marked not only by acts of heroism but also by consistent hard work and intimate knowledge of and concern for his beat. He was characterized by his superiors as a "total officer," one who makes a substantial contribution to his profession through the example he sets. Officer Davis gained the trust and cooperation of many people in the community and managed to solve numerous cases and apprehend suspects when there was little or no information to go on. Preparedness and personal initiative were his hallmarks. This is evidenced by two incidents in which Officer Davis provided prompt medical assistance, at great personal risk, before the arrival of ambulances. One led to the successful delivery of a baby and the other to the saving of a heart attack victim's life.

Among numerous citations, Officer Davis was warmly recommended by his superiors for Officer of the Year, and received a law enforcement scholarship in 1986. A family man and former college fullback, his concern for the community extended into volunteer service with the Big Brother/Big Sister Program.

Officer Paul Fernandez
California Highway Patrol
Modesto, California

On January 28, 1988, at approximately 4:15 P.M., Officer Paul Fernandez joined a vehicle pursuit of a suspect wanted for auto theft. The suspect was armed and under the influence of cocaine at the time, and therefore dangerous. The high-speed chase in Modesto traffic ended when the suspect lost control of his car. The suspect abandoned his vehicle and ran into the office of a nearby inn. When Officer Fernandez and two other policemen pursued him, he grabbed the clerk, held an automatic pistol to her head, and threatened to shoot her. While the suspect struggled with his hostage, Officer Fernandez leaped over the counter, in total disregard for his personal safety, and landed on top of him. With the help of the other officers, the suspect was successfully disarmed and subdued.

On May 24, 1989, Officer Fernandez was awarded the Medal of Valor, the highest honor the state of California can bestow on one of its employees, for his heroic actions. He is a ten-year veteran of the California Highway Patrol.

Detective John Flynn
Suffolk County Police Department
Yaphank, New York

On April 23, 1981, the Suffolk County Police Department received a call to rescue three men trapped inside a 160-foot-high water tank. They had been overcome by fumes while painting the tank's interior, and were lying unconscious at its bottom, dangerously close to a large opening that marked the entrance to a hundred-foot center-support pipe. Worsening weather conditions and fatigue were hampering rescue efforts when Police Officer John Flynn was summoned. Officer Flynn, a highly trained member of the Emergency Services Unit, entered the tank and secured the unconscious workers to prevent their fall, an operation made particularly difficult by darkness and inclement weather. After six hours in the tank he successfully secured two of the workers, but the third fell to his death. Officer Flynn was overcome by fatigue, and only with the encouragement of his fellow officers was he able to survive the ordeal himself.

For personal risk above and beyond the call of duty, Officer Flynn was awarded in 1981 the Medal of Honor, Suffolk County Police Department's highest honor. It was one of many honors received in the course of a distinguished twenty-one-year career with the force. Others include three Bravery Medals, three Meritorious Awards, and one Exceptional Meritorious Award, the District Attorney's Distinguished Service Award for 1988, and the SCDP Patrolmen's Benevolent Association Silver Shield Award for the outstanding Cop of the Year.

Sergeant Randell Guesno
Long Beach Police Department
Long Beach, California

On July 1, 1977, at 9:30 A.M., Sergeant Randell Guesno had just gone off duty and was standing on line at a local branch of the Crocker Bank when he saw a suspicious-looking male come through a door. The man pulled the collar of his sweater over the lower half of his face and started yelling threats and obscenities at those in the bank while waving what appeared to be a shotgun. Positioning himself behind a service counter, Sergeant Guesno pointed his service revolver at the subject and ordered him to drop his weapon. The subject began firing, striking Guesno in the face and leg. Despite his injuries, Sergeant Guesno continued advancing on the suspect and firing until he felt there was no longer a threat. Despite weakening caused by his own injuries, Sergeant Guesno managed to disarm the subject and hold him at gunpoint until paramedics and other police officers arrived. By then the subject had died from wounds he suffered in the exchange, but the bank and its customers were safe.

Sergeant Guesno received the Medal of Valor for risking his own life to protect others and a Purple Heart for the injuries he sustained. In his nineteen years of service, he has won the respect of his comrades and of those he has served in various assignments, including the Jail Division, Patrol Division, Communications Division, and Juvenile Division. His professional response in the bank incident demonstrates that Officer Guesno is truly a police officer twenty-four hours a day.

Sergeant Lillian Impellizeri
City of Charleston Police Department
Charleston, South Carolina

One morning in August 1985 Sergeant Lillian Impellizeri received an urgent call from a home health services nurse who said she had an emergency on her hands. The nurse, who had administered home care to an elderly man three times a week for the past five months, was witnessing a rapid deterioration in the patient's health through the neglect of the daughter who was living with him. The elderly patient had been denied physical therapy and remained bedridden for approximately a year, during which time he had developed bedsores and lost a great deal of weight. The elderly man was also locked in the house with an exterior padlock whenever his daughter was gone. When Sergeant Impellizeri arrived at the premises an hour after the desperate call, she found the man lying on a bed of filth and excrement. He was extremely malnourished and dehydrated. He measured six feet three inches in height but he weighed only eighty-seven pounds! Officer Impellizeri arranged for the patient to be transported by EMS technicians to the hospital and treated. Then she investigated the appropriate criminal charges that could be brought against the daughter. After diligent research in the state codes, Sergeant Impellizeri found a criminal statute concerning abuse and neglect of adults which had been enacted in 1974 but not enforced.

A 13-year veteran of the City of Charleston Police Force, Sergeant Impellizeri has gained considerable national acclaim for her leadership on the issue of abuse of the elderly. She helped secure a federal grant to help combat the victimization of elderly people and set up an Elder Supportline to give assistance to senior citizens. Sergeant Impellizeri was honored by *Parade* magazine as one of the Top Ten Police Officers of the year in 1986 and by the Kiwanis Club as Citizen of the Year in 1985.

Sergeant Dennis Keogh
Kettering Police Department
Kettering, Ohio

The murder of Theresa Lauricella in her bedroom in the early morning hours of August 18, 1972, set off an intensive police investigation that led to the arrest of three suspects on charges of first degree murder. Detective Dennis Keogh led that investigation and brought Theresa Lauricella's killers to justice. As often happens, this case was far from over after the arrest of the suspects. It took more than a year of legal maneuvering and three jury trials, extensively covered by the local news media, before two of the suspects were convicted and given life sentences for their participation in the brutal homicide A third suspect was found not guilty by a jury. The convictions were achieved through the solid and tireless policework of Detective Dennis Keogh, who not only carried the burden of the investigation, but also shared the state's table and testified at all three trials.

In this and many other cases, Detective Keogh distinguished himself by his investigative zeal, his attention to detail, and his willingness to devote off-duty hours to the gathering and preparation of evidence. A U.S. Air Force veteran, Detective Keogh has been with the Kettering Police Department since 1967. He has been involved with the department's Special Response Team as a hostage negotiator and was administrator of the K9 program, in recognition of which he recently received the Kettering Optimist's Policeman of the Year Award.

Officer Clarence R. Kirk
Houston Police Department
Houston, Texas

A ten-year veteran of the Houston Police Department, Officer Clarence R. Kirk has been instrumental in the department's efforts to reduce the fear of crime among Houston residents. His work in this area began in 1982 with his appointment to the Fear Reduction Task Force, which was established in response to a National Institute of Justice initiative for calming the fear of crime among citizens throughout the country. To this assignment Officer Kirk brought first-hand knowledge of the fear of crime, having witnessed its effects on citizens in the department's North Shepherd substation, which he patrolled. He also developed new ways to enhance the task force's overall objectives. Officer Kirk sought to create environments in which citizens would feel comfortable sharing information about neighborhood crime with their local police. In November 1983, chiefly through the initiative of Officer Kirk, the department's first police community center opened its doors, offering a variety of programs designed to encourage citizen participation in efforts to fight crime, including the organization of civic clubs, interaction with area schools, and the formation of a minister's alliance to distribute information through churches and recreational programs.

In 1984 Officer Kirk received the Houston Police Department's Officer of the Year Award for his role in establishing community policing centers. The centers, and Officer Kirk's work there, have become internationally recognized for their effectiveness. Delegations from as far away as Great Britain, Japan, Mexico, and Switzerland have toured the model community centers to see how they have helped to solve numerous neighborhood crimes.

Officer David Magnusson
Dade County Police Department
Miami, Florida

In his short career with the Miami Police, Officer David Magnusson has emerged as a kind of one-man war on drugs. As a patrol officer in one of Miami's most notorious drug-infested areas, he made an astonishing 230 felony and 68 misdemeanor arrests for street narcotics sales in 1988 alone, many of them involving armed and dangerous suspects. To this end, Officer Magnusson has employed various tactics, including "park-and-walk," during which he parks his police car and patrols his assigned zone on foot. This enables him more effectively to locate and break up small narcotics deals and other crimes in progress, no small feat. Officer Magnusson's initiative has yielded impressive results in the fight against crack houses, usually abandoned buildings favored by drug dealers and users. As a result of his efforts the city of Miami has instituted an ongoing program to identify and raze these structures.

Only twenty-seven years old, Officer Magnusson is one of the most honored members of the Miami Police Department. In 1988 he won the department's Most Outstanding Officer of the Month Award twice and his patrol shift's Officer of the Month Award five times. In his four years with the department, he has amassed over thirty commendations for outstanding performance of duty. And in recognition of his personal drive and commitment to community service, Officer Magnusson was named the Miami Police Department's 1988 Officer of the Year.

Officer Robert M. Martinez
Austin Police Department
Austin, Texas

While assigned to the Organized Crime and the Hispanic Crime Units, Senior Patrol Officer Robert M. Martinez was able to enlist the cooperation of Interpol and the attorney general of the Republic of Mexico in an effort to extradite fifteen Mexican nationals suspected of committing murders in Texas. Gaining Mexican cooperation is an especially notable achievement, as Mexico does not normally allow the extradition of criminals. As a member of the highly acclaimed Hispanic Crime Unit, Officer Martinez was responsible for investigating all robbery and homicide cases that involved Mexican nationals, and was able to clear about two hundred robberies in which the victims were undocumented workers. In 1989 he also helped form Citizens Helping Austin Neighborhood Gang Environment (CHANGE), a citizens' group dedicated to reducing gang activity in the community.

In honor of Officer Martinez's professionalism in dealing with crime in the Hispanic community, Las Fiestas Patrias of Austin passed a resolution declaring September 16, 1988, Robert Martinez Day. His son, Robbie Martinez, Jr., also an officer with the Austin Department, died in a car accident in the spring of 1989, after which the city council officially renamed a street Martinez Street, in the section of town where the elder Martinez grew up. It is a tribute to a distinguished career dedicated to making Austin a better and safer place.

Officer Armand G. Ouellette
Metropolitan Police Department
Boston, Massachusetts

On May 6, 1983, a valve malfunctioned at the Deer Island Sewage Treatment Plant, flooding the control silo and dumping raw sewage into Boston Harbor. Officer Armand G. Ouellette, a voluntary member of the Metropolitan Police Department's Underwater Rescue and Recovery Unit, was summoned to the scene of the emergency, and over a forty-eight hour period, dived repeatedly into six million gallons of raw sewage, exposing himself to high temperatures and pockets of poisonous gas. Battling zero visibility and physical illness triggered by the fumes, Officer Ouellette managed eventually to find his way through a maze of pipes and valves to locate the source of the problem. He then manually cranked the control valve over four hundred times, successfully closing off the leak and averting a major environmental and economic disaster to coastal communities. More recently, in 1986, Officer Ouellette happened upon smoke and flames coming from the fourth floor of a tenement occupied by elderly residents. After making the appropriate notifications, he single-handedly, and at great personal risk, cleared the building of its residents.

These two actions demonstrate Officer Ouellette's quick thinking and determination in the face of danger. A sixteen-year veteran of the department, he was a patrol officer in several districts before volunteering for the Tactical Operations Patrol Squad Unit (TOPS), organized in 1975. Of second-generation French descent, the bilingual Ouellette served on nuclear submarines in the U.S. Navy and holds a B.A. in psychology and a master's degree in criminal justice.

Senior Corporal James R. Pool
Dallas Police Department
Dallas, Texas

On the night of July 8, 1986, Corporal James R. Pool was off duty in his car when he happened upon a fiery collision on a major Dallas interstate highway. An eighteen-wheel tractor trailer had crashed into the rear of a vehicle that had slowed because a cow was crossing the highway. The large truck, which had been traveling at a speed in excess of 80 mph literally embedded itself in the back of the vehicle and started a fire that shot flames a hundred feet into the air. Upon his arrival at the scene, Corporal Pool immediately risked his life in an attempt to save an elderly couple who were trapped and unconscious in their burning vehicle. While struggling to rescue them, an explosion from a ruptured fuel tank knocked Corporal Pool and another officer to the pavement. Against great odds and with repeated efforts, Corporal Pool and two other officers succeeded in extracting the woman from the burning car and administered emergency aid to her. However, the valiant efforts of Corporal Pool and his colleagues to rescue the husband were in vain.

Corporal Pool was awarded the Medal of Valor and a Lifesaving Award for his heroic efforts in this incident. He was also named Departmental Officer of the Year and Outstanding Officer of 1987. As a patrolman, Corporal Pool led his sector in felony arrests. In 1988 he was assigned to the Dallas office of the FBI as part of the DPD/FBI General Property Crimes Task Force, for which he received an FBI Letter of Commendation for Performance by Director William Sessions. A sixteen-year veteran of the force, he is currently class advisor at the Police Academy.

Officer Arthur N. Sapp
Colorado Springs Police Department
Colorado Springs, Colorado

"Art Sapp's School of Pain" — that's what some call Officer Arthur N. Sapp's officer survival classes, and he will be the last to deny it. Says Officer Sapp, "The pain you feel working out is nothing compared to the real pain you'll feel in the streets." He has traveled throughout the country teaching his courses on defensive tactics to over six thousand law enforcement and military personnel. In the course he demonstrates hand-to-hand combat, use of the PR24 Police Baton, and arrest control techniques. With a black belt in tae kwon do and a brown belt in judo, he is an expert in the use of force. However, his primary concern is teaching officers to use humane and effective techniques when force is necessary. Officer Sapp is dedicated to educating the public as well as law enforcement officials. He has taught rape prevention and self-defense courses, and spoken at schools and community centers on safety concerns. Officer Sapp is often accompanied by his partner, police dog Axel. They work as a team training prospective K9 officers.

In his fourteen-year career with the CSPD, Officer Sapp has been a member of the Tactical Enforcement Unit (TEU), the Specialized Criminal Apprehension Team (SCAT), and the Special Anti-Crime Squads (SACS). Officer Sapp has received numerous commendations and honors, including the 1988 Albert J. Grazioli Award for his outstanding contribution to criminal justice training.

Officer Richard Schmidt
Saint Paul Police Department
Saint Paul, Minnesota

On July 18, 1985, two patrol officers responded to a call that a young man already wanted for felonious assault and possession of a deadly weapon was allegedly holding a knife to someone's throat. When they arrived at the scene, the suspect fled across a yard, commandeered a truck, and finally holed up in a house a few blocks away. When Officer Richard Schmidt and another officer arrived and entered the house, they found the suspect holding a young boy hostage. The man attacked Officer Schmidt, managed to steal his service revolver, and wounded two officers. At great personal risk, Officer Schmidt wrested control of his weapon away from the criminal and wounded the felon fatally. Had Officer Schmidt not disabled the suspect, the strong possibility existed that he would have shot other officers in his attempts to evade arrest.

For his actions in this case, Officer Schmidt was awarded the Saint Paul Police Department's Medal of Valor on October 25, 1985. In addition, he was named 1985 Police Officer of the Year, the high point of a distinguished career that began in 1955.

Sergeant William G. Spalding
Prince George's County Police Department
Prince George's County, Maryland

In the early 1970s Sergeant William G. Spalding was at the scene of a possible burglary in progress in which an officer had already been killed. Officers were scouring the building when one of them fired at an unknown target. His actions triggered a barrage of shots from the other officers. In all, more than a hundred shots were fired by the officers, even though there turned out to be no target or hostile party in evidence. Fortunately, no one was injured in this incident, but it convinced Sergeant William Spalding, a twenty-four-year veteran of the department, that such an uncontrolled response to a violent act was a serious problem, especially at a time of rising terrorist threats. Sergeant Spalding campaigned tirelessly for the development of a Crisis Management Team concept to be implemented at high risk incidents. In 1976 he was asked to create and train the first component of this team — the Emergency Services Team. Over the next thirteen years, he further developed the project, trained the first Negotiating Team and On-Scene Commanders, and led the team in over 250 barricade incidents. The Prince George's Conflict Management Team is now world-renowned and has been featured on "60 Minutes," "All Things Considered," and a BBC special production on international terrorism. Sergeant Spalding has trained twenty-eight groups from sixteen different countries as a part of a congressionally-funded Terrorism Assistance Program for foreign police departments.

Detective John Winston Stem, Sr.
Baltimore County Police Department
Baltimore, Maryland

On July 6, 1977, Officer John Winston Stem, Sr., responded as a backup to a call concerning a disorderly juvenile. The first officer on the scene had been struck in the head by a round from a high-powered rifle. Two other officers also came under fire. Officer Stem fired at the sniper from a covered position, enabling an officer to rescue his injured colleague, who lay on the street beside his cruiser. As Stem ran between houses to assist them, he came under heavy fire and was wounded. The bullet lodged in his spine, paralyzing him from the waist down.

As a result of his heroic efforts, Officer Stem was awarded the Baltimore County Police Department's highest award, the Medal of Honor, only the sixth officer to receive it in the department's one-hundred-year history. An outpouring of community support, totaling over $30,000, enabled Officer Stem's family to build a special house to accommodate the special needs produced by his injury. Though eligible for a medical pension, Officer Stem notified his department that he intended to return to work in some capacity. Sixteen months and many grueling physical therapy sessions later, Officer Stem did just that. At first he was assigned to the Youth Services Division as a counselor for problem youths, but he longed to return to investigative work. Subsequently he directed his energies toward finding runaway and abducted children. Though confined to a wheelchair, Officer Stem has been directly involved in the investigation of approximately seventy child abduction cases, all of which resulted in the safe return of the child. In the more than twelve years since his injury, Officer Stem has overcome monumental odds with impressive determination and has been an inspiration to his fellow officers and to the community.

Lieutenant Loren E. Stevens
Las Vegas Metropolitan Police Department
Las Vegas, Nevada

In 1984 Las Vegas crime reached new heights, making the city third in the nation in terms of crime. The newly elected sheriff challenged members of the police department to come up with new and innovative approaches to crime fighting. None was more successful than Lieutenant Loren E. Stevens. He proposed that law enforcement officials cooperate more effectively with the business community and private citizens. As police department funds and manpower were extremely limited, he selected a group of six highly experienced officers and, with private donations, formed the Special Trust Investigative Fund (STIF), a tax-exempt corporation dedicated to undertaking highly sophisticated sting operations. Using electronic surveillance equipment and an elaborate operational facade, undercover officers were able to penetrate the inner circles of organized crime for the first time in years. Officer Stevens and his squad proceeded to trap and arrest 513 criminals involved in 1,797 felony cases, including such charges as credit card fraud, counterfeiting, and bank embezzlement. The sting group had an astonishing 98 percent conviction rate due to the airtight evidence they provided. From 1984 to 1988 the Las Vegas area dropped from its position as number three in national crime to number sixty-five, thanks largely to the innovative ideas of Lieutenant Stevens and the accomplishments of his team.

Officer Austin Ware
Chicago Police Department
Chicago, Illinois

On December 5, 1985, Officer Austin Ware, who was off duty at the time, was entering a restaurant when he confronted a man armed with a .45-caliber pistol who was in the process of stealing money from customers and threatening the cashiers. Officer Ware walked up behind the offender and stated he was a cop. In an ensuing struggle, the offender grabbed the officer's service revolver. Officer Ware fired a shot which struck, but failed to stop, the robber. After firing two more shots, the officer was finally able to disarm the subject, who was fatally wounded. It was only then that Officer Ware realized he was himself seriously injured. He subsequently underwent emergency surgery.

Officer Ware's actions, taken at great risk to his own person, possibly prevented other patrons and employees of the restaurant from being injured or killed during the robbery attempt. For this action, Officer Ware received the Superintendent's Award of Valor, the Police Medal and the Police Blue Star Award, adding to an already impressive list of commendations. An officer since 1973, Ware has made more than one thousand arrests and is one of the most highly decorated members of the force.

Police Dog Zach (deceased)
K9 Unit, King County Police Department
Seattle, Washington

On July 7, 1988, police dog Zach was shot and killed in the line of duty while tracking a fleeing felon who was wanted on a variety of criminal charges in Salt Lake City. Zach and his handler encountered the suspect in heavy brush near the Seattle-Tacoma International Airport. While Zach was wrestling the suspect to the ground, the man opened fire, fatally wounding the four-and-a half-year-old German shepherd. Zach continued struggling, and the suspect died from the firing of his own gun during the altercation. Zach's bravery is not surprising. It ran in his blood. His father, Jake, was shot while chasing bank robbers several years ago, and now lives in retirement.

At his funeral, Zach was eulogized for his bravery as one "who taught his fellow police officers how to do a tough job in a hostile environment but also one who loved to chase rabbits and play with children." In his years on the force, Zach regularly pursued suspects, capturing more than one hundred fifty of them, and was involved in narcotic searches. As well, he was a frequent visitor to Seattle classrooms, where he demonstrated canine skills to groups of wide-eyed children.

Mike Levy/Seattle Times

The National Law Enforcement Memorial

In October 1989 construction began on a unique monument in the nation's capital. Just a short distance from the Mall and Capitol Hill, the three-acre park will be America's first National Law Enforcement Memorial. When it is completed at the end of 1990, the memorial, that was authorized by a 1984 act of the U.S. Congress, will be an oasis for reflection upon the extraordinary sacrifice and commitment of this nation's police officers. Both the dead and living will be honored there for their selflessness and for their exploits.

The Memorial's "pathway of remembrance" will form an oval-shaped border for the carefully landscaped grounds. Polished granite walls, bearing the names of fallen law enforcement officers, will edge the tree-lined pathway. Names of officers killed in future years will be added annually.

A police officer does not have to die to become a hero. It's the way that an officer lives and serves that defines one. Vivian Eney, president of Concerns of Police Survivors (COPS), and the widow of a fallen police officer, has repeatedly reminded us of this. Yet, until now, those brave men and women who have risked their lives and given so much to their communities and to the nation have received surprisingly little thanks in return.

Like this book, the National Law Enforcement Memorial will let the families and friends of fallen officers know the nation appreciates their contributions. It will honor the living as well as those who have given their lives. And like *Tribute*, the Memorial will celebrate America's finest.

Larry Olsen

Policing the Future

What will police life be like in the year 2000 and beyond? Will cops mirror the popular movie depiction of Robocop, a high-tech law enforcer employed by a private enterprise to wage war against crime? Will he be like that wholesome officer in the Norman Rockwell painting, patrolling a world of total goodness and apple pie? Or will tomorrow's cop be pretty much the same, continuing to fight an uphill battle against drugs, crime, violence, and poverty? More than likely, tomorrow's cop will be equal parts of all of these. But he'll also probably be a better-educated and more efficient ombudsman and representative of the government.

New information technologies have probably had the greatest impact on policework in the last decade and will continue to do so in the future. Law enforcement agencies first began using computers in the mid-1960s to manage financial operations and to store criminal records. The ability to check criminal history and determine whether a person was "wanted" in just minutes was a source of amazement to veteran officers. Now sophisticated computer systems ride in patrol cars, giving officers the ability to access a wide variety of information in seconds. In St. Petersburg, Florida, officers use personal lap-top computers and cellular phones to enter and transfer data immediately. Many cities are installing enhanced 911 systems that access emergency communications centers and automatically show police the location of the call. And patrol cars are increasingly equipped with automatic vehicle locaters that monitor the exact position of a patrol car so that if it's in trouble, help can be swiftly dispatched.

Information technology has enhanced crime-solving capabilities as well. Computer data banks and sophisticated programs enable crime-analysis personnel to discern crime patterns. Automated fingerprint identification systems make suspect identification easier. And dramatic advances are being realized in "genetic fingerprinting," a method of identifying criminals by matching their unique DNA structure to body fluids or a strand of hair left at a crime scene.

Police in Baltimore County, Maryland, Tucson, Arizona, and Charlotte, North Carolina, are developing "expert investigative systems" that team experienced detectives with sophisticated computer systems to reduce the time involved in identifying criminals and solving crimes.

Two decades of research show that basic police strategies for deterring and solving crimes — random preventive patrol, rapid response to crime calls, and criminal investigations — are limited in their effectiveness. The police of the future will be searching for approaches that are more efficient and productive.

Problem-oriented policing is one such approach. Professor Herman Goldstein of the University of Wisconsin at Madison first described the concept in a 1979 article in Crime and Delinquency. He wrote that the traditional police function was to respond to persistent problems identified by citizens who turn to them for assistance. Goldstein suggested that police would be more successful if they analyzed all the incidents together to identify common problems and trends of crime. Once they understood the underlying conditions that generate crime, they could work hand in hand with the public and the business community to develop long-term solutions.

A look at existing crime patterns readily shows the promise of problem-oriented policing. More often than not, police are dealing with repeat incidents of crime — the same people, the same locations. About 60 percent of crime calls originate from about 10 percent of the addresses in the city. Ten percent of the victims account for 40 percent of the reported crimes, and 10 percent of the criminals are responsible for about 55 percent of the offenses. In the problem-oriented policing approach, officers are expected to detect these repeat incidents and patterns of crime and to design a community-based strategy to eliminate them.

Under a grant from the National Institute of Justice, with technical assistance from the Police Executive Research Forum, the Newport News, Virginia, Police Department began a problem-oriented policing program in 1985. Some examples from this pilot project illustrate the effectiveness of problem-oriented policing. For several weeks, police had been getting calls about rowdy kids committing vandalism in a neighborhood near a roller skating rink. An officer used problem-solving methods to stop such incidents. He analyzed the situation and discovered that the youths only became rowdy and destructive while walking home after the rink had closed. It turned out they were hoofing it home because no transportation was available to get them to and from the rink. After this was brought to the rink owners attention, he arranged for bus service, and the vandalism quickly ceased.

In another example, theft from cars in a parking lot was dramatically reduced when a police officer assessed the situation and recommended improved lighting and security. Such systematic approaches to crime are already being applied successfully in a number of cities across the nation.

The problem-oriented policing approach is also being applied to the drug problem in five large cities, with support from the Bureau of Justice Assistance. A public housing project in Tulsa, Oklahoma, experienced a decline of over 70 percent in violent crime after officers began using problem-solving techniques. In San Diego, California, patrol officers applied such techniques to a drug-infested apartment complex with major success. Another officer in San Diego was able to rid the city of a drug den that had been operating for years in a residential area.

Future police leaders will have to take some bold steps, particularly in the areas of minority concerns and of education and training. They will need to continue aggressively promoting the employment of minorities and women and to insure that departments increasingly reflect the racial composition of the communities in which they serve. And tomorrow's leaders will have to make sure that their officers are as well educated and trained as they are equipped technically. Currently, great variations exist in police policies. Although many in law enforcement acknowledge the importance of education, only 14 percent of the police departments in the United States require any education beyond high school. And few require college work for promotion. As for police training, the differences are equally stark. Florida requires a minimum of four hundred hours of entry level training for police officer certification while Kansas requires only two hundred. In Lakewood, Colorado, a police officer must have a college degree, while Denver, Colorado, only requires a high school diploma. These differences in local policy will obviously affect the future of policing and create a patchwork of approaches.

The force of the future will have to be well trained in the new technologies. The use of computer-assisted instruction will make such training easier, as officers can learn at their own pace and without major interruptions in duty assignments. Television programs will likely become a key method of instruction. Private enterprise has already created a Law Enforcement Television Network (LETN) and is marketing its twenty-four hour coverage on law enforcement issues and training to police departments nationwide.

The police organization of the future will be more horizontal in structure than the traditional military model and will have perhaps three or four levels of command rather than eight to ten. It will be highly decentralized to accommodate the problem-oriented police approach. Each supervisor will oversee fifteen to twenty officers who will operate as fairly independent agents in their areas of assignment. The ratio of police officers to citizens will significantly decline. Increasingly, civilians will be employed for many police tasks that are not strictly law enforcement. These civilians will work in all areas of the police organization. Street patrol officers will work closely with civilian teams that possess a variety of skills, including a problem analyst, a neighborhood organizer, a volunteer coordinator, and a liaison with other governmental services. These police and civilian teams will effectively coordinate the delivery of a range of governmental services that affect the quality of life in the community.

How the police officer of the future spends the day on the beat is not yet in sharp focus. We have no crystal ball. The officer's future will be designed by the actions and resolve of today's law enforcement leaders. Some of those leaders envision a future filled with problems. They yearn for better days and yet fail to push aggressively for reform. Others imagine the immense opportunities and challenges that lie ahead, and they eagerly proceed to pioneer methods and technologies that will diminish future crime problems. The police officer of today walks a heady beat — along the threshold of a fresh decade and a new century.

— Darrel Stephens

Acknowledgments

In the four years of creating *Tribute* an awesome amount of Australian-American logistical planning occurred that involved literally hundreds of people from throughout the world. This book would not be a reality without their support and assistance. The following is a list of most of these special people. Our apologies to anyone we might have inadvertently omitted.

In Sydney, Australia, our special thanks to Dr. Sherly Snyman for coordinating operations from Down Under; to Shona Hammond for transcribing the original police interviews; to Alex, Basil, and Marti Snymann for their assistance and liaison between Sydney, the States and beyond; and, to James Fraser for some obscure reason.

In London, a big thanks goes to Jim Henderson of Pen Graphics, whose creative support was a catalyst to the project.

And in the United States, our hats go off to practically the entire American public which greeted our project with open arms. Thanks to Fallon, Nomi and Jabez, Jacobs and Zinns, Lenny and Carole Grau, Grau & Weiner, Phil and Angelo Melito, Christine Demetro, and Maria del Carmen Sarmiento for their assistance to weary and confused travelers. Also special thanks to Rick Wallace (for his keen judgement of photography) and David Branson of Kaye Scholer, Fierman, Hays & Handler; to Charles Nichols of Nicholstone for his flexible approach to binding deadlines; to Billy Prince, president of the Law Enforcement Television Network; to Dewey Stokes, president of the Fraternal Order of Police, for FOP's assistance in reaching the vast network of members, as well as to all of the other police organizations that have contributed.

And, finally, our deep appreciation goes to Darrel Stephens and the staff of PERF and to all the U.S. law enforcement groups and individuals who helped arrange access for the *Tribute* photographers to shoot throughout the country. Without their extraordinary efforts, *Tribute* would simply not exist.

Sydney, Australia

Ann and Tony Lawrence
Jim Wells
Brian Agnew
John Tier
Ian Anderson
Katy and Jock Young
Dick and Dora Manclark
Isis Skelly
Keith Chesswell

Melbourne, Australia

Lou Wong
Jane Ballantyne
Rita Hookem
Anita Koning
Staff of Image Bank, Melbourne
Geff Moorfoot
Simon and Pam Greenwood
Witch Type
Sandy Scott
Bob Campion
John McIver
The Moore Family
John Bickford

Perth, Australia

Annabel and Alan Croker
Jim Johnson
Roger Taylor
Mike Carter

London, England

Pen Graphics
Mervyn Nash
Julian Coles

United States of America

Tribute Photographers

John Bauguess
Todd Buchanan
Joe Cantrell
Aaron Chang
Gary S. Chapman
Gary L. Gaynor
Carol Guzy
Peter Hendrie
Jeff Jacobson
Brennon Jones
Robert F. Kusel
Paul McIver
Howard Moss
Patrick Tehan
Mark S. Wexler
Lee Zaichick

Friends

Tony Anthony
Nina Barnett
Jean Castelli
Don Davidson
Stefan Ensler
C.W. Griffith
Charlie Hewitt
Ethan Hoffman
Mike Keating
David Leeson
Susan Maitland
Paul Mathieson
Nate and Marjorie Rosenblatt
Mark Rykoff
Brian Smith
Jim Walpole
David Walters
Todd Weinstein
Rob Wilson

Police Executive Research Forum

Dawn Blackburn
Sheila Bodner
Jennifer Brooks
Sally Chalmers
Tia Clark
Julie Cowan
John Eck
William Geller
Sandra Gray
Sheldon Greenberg
Diane Hill
Clifford Karchmer
Chris Leahy
Martha Plotkin
Karin Schmerler
Michael Scott
John Stedman
Darrel Stephens
Dan Stern
Lexta Taylor
Deborah Weisel

U.S. Police Departments

Alexandria, VA Police Dept.
Chief Gary Leonard

Anchorage, AK Police Dept.
Chief Kevin O'Leary
Fran Turney
Sgt. Walt Monegan
Officer Dave Brown
Sgt. Chris Miller

Atlanta, GA Police Division
Commissioner George Napper
Chief Morris G. Redding

Austin, TX Police Dept.
Chief Jim Everett
Carol C. Benson
Lt. Pete Taylor

Baltimore County, MD Police Dept.
Chief Cornelius J. Behan
Col. Leonard Supenski

Boca Raton, FL Police Dept.
Chief Peter A. Petracco

Boise, ID Police Dept.
Chief James Carvino
Officer Angela Bevier
Det. Merlin Lords
Lt. Richard Linderer
Susie Boring

Boston, MA Police Dept.
Commissioner Francis Roache

CA Highway Patrol
Commissioner M.J. Hannigan

Casper, WY Police Dept.
Chief Fred W. Rainguet
Division Comdr. Michael Colling
Officer Pat Eastes

Charleston, SC Police Dept.
Chief Reuben M. Greenberg

Charlotte, NC Police Dept.
Chief S.H. Killman

Chicago, IL Police Dept.
Supt. LeRoy Martin
Sgt. Johnnie Bully
Officer Charles Swanson
Comdr. Ettore De Vito
Comdr. Nelson S. Barreto
Tina Vicini
Jackie Kimber

Cincinnati, OH Police Division
Chief Lawrence Whalen
Officer Howard Nichols
Sgt. Dick Newsom
Sgt. David Hall
Officer Gary Fritsch
Officer Don Murnan

Clearwater, FL Police Dept.
Chief Sid Klein

Colorado Springs, CO Police Dept.
Chief James D. Munger
Acting Chief J. Pat McElderry

Dallas, TX Police Dept.
Chief Mack M. Vines
Chief Robert Jackson
Asst. Chief Sam Gonzalez
Mr. Ed Spencer
Sgt. James Chandler
Officer John Henry James
Lt. Jill Muncy

Detroit, MI Police Dept.
Chief William L. Hart
Lt. Phil Foster

El Paso, TX Police Dept.
Chief John E. Scagno
Lt. J.R. Grijalva
Sgt. Andres Yslas
Officer Luis E. Barrio
Officer Victor Colunga
Officer Vasquez

Eugene, OR Police Services Division
Deputy Chief John D. Rutledge
Capt. Richard M. Loveall
Lt. Ellwood H. Cushman
Police Agent Dennis A. Williams
Officer Stanley Reeves
Officer Kenneth W. Saxon, III
Officer Anthony D. Veach
Scott A. Cushman

Evanston, IL Police Dept.
Chief Ernest A. Jacobi

Fairfax County, VA Police Dept.
Chief John E. Granfield

Fayetteville, NC Police Dept.
Chief Ronald Hansen
Kelly R. Thompson

Ft. Lauderdale, FL Police Dept.
Chief Joseph C. Gerwens
Sgt. Greg Kridos
Officer Jorge Benitez-Merlo
Officer Eddie Evarts
Officer William Lumm
Officer Barry Margolis
Officer Marty Schutt
Officer William Spodnick
Officer Wayne Swenson
Officer Chuck Wischer
Officer Joe Diaz
Officer Mike Kent
Officer Dan Ashley
Col. Dunne

Honolulu, HI Police Dept.
Chief Douglas G. Gibb
Asst. Chief Robert Kane
Asst. Chief Ersel Kilburn
Maj. Herbert Okemura

Capt. Robert Thomas
Lt. Wayne Goodwin
Lt. James Souza
Sgt. Harold Evangelista
Sgt. Charles Lacaden
Sgt. Roger Lau
Benson Nakamura
Officer Leith Anderson
Officer Gary Faria
Officer Bernard Kaopuiki
Officer Herbert Nakamura
Officer Elroy Paikai
Officer Mark Tanga
Officer Charles Wiggins
"King"
Officer Jean Motoyama Fujimoto

Houston, TX Police Dept.
Chief Lee P. Brown

Kansas City, MO Police Dept.
Chief Larry Joiner
Maj. David Barton
Capt. Gary Chapman
Sgt. Louis Zacharias
Lt. Col. Floyd Bartch
Officer James Svoboda
Officer Anthony Ell
Lt. Col. Michael Boyle
Sgt. Dan Molloy

Kettering, OH Police Dept.
Chief James M. O'Dell

King County, WA Police Dept.
Sheriff Jim Montgomery
Sgt. Leigh McGougan
Officer Randy Gehrke
Police Dog "Zach"
Officer Steve Wandel
Police Dog "Luke"
Sgt. Bill Dickinson

Lakewood, CO Police Dept.
Chief Charles Johnston
Lt. Alan C. Youngs
Agent Catherine Barnes
Agent Gregg Bramblett
Agent Jerry Hamilton
Sgt. Jerry Garner

Las Vegas, NV Metropolitan Police Dept.
Sheriff John Moran
Deputy Chief John L. Sullivan
Undersheriff Eric S. Cooper
Lt. Robert Chinn
Lt. Bill Young
Sgt. Ken Caldwell